THE LIBRARY OF HOLOCAUST TESTIMONIES

My Child is Back!

The Library of Holocaust Testimonies

Editors: Antony Polonsky, Sir Martin Gilbert CBE, Aubrey Newman,
Raphael F. Scharf, Ben Helfgott MBE

Under the auspices of the Yad Vashem Committee of the Board of
Deputies of British Jews and the Centre for Holocaust Studies,
University of Leicester

My Child is Back!

URSULA PAWEL

VALLENTINE MITCHELL
LONDON • PORTLAND, OR

First published in 2000 by
VALLENTINE MITCHELL

ISBS, 920 NE 58th Avenue, Suite 300
Portland, Oregon 97213-3786

Suite 314, Premier House
Edgware, Middlesex HA8 7BJ

www.vmbooks.com

British Library Cataloguing in Publication Data
Pawel, Ursula
    My child is back!. – (The library of Holocaust testimonies)
    1. Pawel, Ursula 2. Jews – Germany – Biography 3. Jewish
    children in the Holocaust 4. Holocaust, Jewish (1939–1945) –
    Personal narratives
    I. Title
    940.5'318

ISBN 978 0 85303 404 9
ISSN 1363-3759

Library of Congress Cataloging-in-Publication Data
Pawel, Ursula, 1926 –
    My child is back! / Ursula Pawel
        p.cm. – (Library of Holocaust Testimonies)
    ISBN 0-85303-404-4 (pbk).
        1. Pawel, Ursula, 1926 – 2. Jews – Germany – History –
    1933–1945. 3. Children of interfaith marriage – Germany –
    Biography. 4. Holocaust, Jewish (1939–1945) – Germany –
    Personal narratives. 5. Germany – Biography. I. Title. II. Series.

DS135.G5 P39 2000
940.53'18'092 – dc21
[B]   00–056618

Printed by Edwards Brothers Inc, Ann Arbor, MI

I dedicate this book
to the memory of
my father and my brother,
and my friends and relatives
who perished.

Contents

List of Illustrations

Biographical Note

Ursula Pawel was born in 1926 in Germany as the daughter of a Christian mother and a Jewish father. In 1942 she was sent to a concentration camp. Her father and her brother died in Auschwitz but, ironically, her life was saved by two German soldiers. Liberated in 1945, she was reunited with her mother ('My Child is Back!') and they came to America in 1947. Her dream of becoming a physician was out of reach, but following her training as an X-ray technologist she worked in that field for many years. Her husband, who died in 1999, was a professor of engineering. She has two sons and one granddaughter.

The Library of Holocaust Testimonies

Ten years have passed since Frank Cass launched his Library of Holocaust Testimonies. It was greatly to his credit that this was done, and even more remarkable that it has continued and flourished. The memoirs of each survivor throw new light and cast new perspectives on the fate of the Jews of Europe during the Holocaust. No voice is too small or humble to be heard, no story so familiar that it fails to tell the reader something new, something hitherto unnoticed, something previously unknown.

Each new memoir adds to our knowledge not only of the Holocaust, but also of many aspects of the human condition that are universal and timeless: the power of evil and the courage of the oppressed; the cruelty of the bystanders and the heroism of those who sought to help, despite the risks; the part played by family and community; the question of who knew what and when; the responsibility of the wider world for the destructive behaviour of tyrants and their henchmen.

Fifty memoirs are already in print in the Library of Holocaust Testimonies, and several more are being published each year. In this way anyone interested in the Holocaust will be able to draw upon a rich seam of eyewitness accounts. They can also use another Vallentine Mitchell publication, the multi-volume *Holocaust Memoir Digest*, edited by Esther Goldberg, to explore the contents of survivor memoirs in a way that makes them particularly accessible to teachers and students alike.

Sir Martin Gilbert
London, April 2005

Introduction

My sons asked me a long time ago to write my life-story, but I think it was my old friend Buschi's (Hilde Buschhoff's) death which finally motivated me to give it a try.

Right after my liberation in 1945, even when I was still on the road to my aunt's house in West Germany, I began making some notes of my experiences. I expanded the account with dates and details into a record, and wrote it all into a beautiful little scrapbook my aunt gave me shortly after I got to her house, and which I still treasure. Without these notes it would have been impossible for me to recall in detail the events of my life, especially those in the camps from 1942 to 1947.

So here then is my story from my childhood in Germany to my early days in America. I have written it for my sons, David and Bruce, but without the encouragement, guidance, criticism and help of my husband it would not have come to fruition.

URSULA PAWEL (NÉE LENNEBERG):

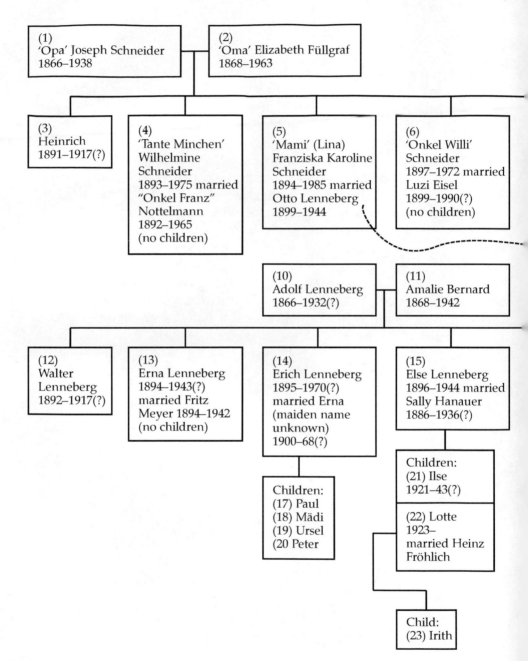

(1) 'Opa' Joseph Schneider 1866–1938

(2) 'Oma' Elizabeth Füllgraf 1868–1963

(3) Heinrich 1891–1917(?)

(4) 'Tante Minchen' Wilhelmine Schneider 1893–1975 married "Onkel Franz" Nottelmann 1892–1965 (no children)

(5) 'Mami' (Lina) Franziska Karoline Schneider 1894–1985 married Otto Lenneberg 1899–1944

(6) 'Onkel Willi' Schneider 1897–1972 married Luzi Eisel 1899–1990(?) (no children)

(10) Adolf Lenneberg 1866–1932(?)

(11) Amalie Bernard 1868–1942

(12) Walter Lenneberg 1892–1917(?)

(13) Erna Lenneberg 1894–1943(?) married Fritz Meyer 1894–1942 (no children)

(14) Erich Lenneberg 1895–1970(?) married Erna (maiden name unknown) 1900–68(?)

(15) Else Lenneberg 1896–1944 married Sally Hanauer 1886–1936(?)

Children:
(17) Paul
(18) Mädi
(19) Ursel
(20 Peter

Children:
(21) Ilse 1921–43(?)

(22) Lotte 1923– married Heinz Fröhlich

Child:
(23) Irith

FAMILY TREE

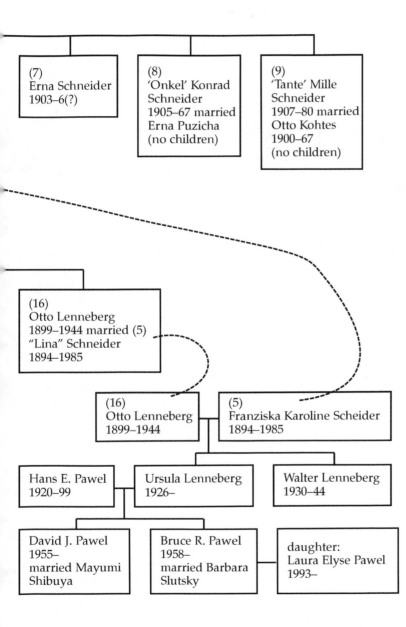

(7)
Erna Schneider
1903–6(?)

(8)
'Onkel' Konrad
Schneider
1905–67 married
Erna Puzicha
(no children)

(9)
'Tante' Mille
Schneider
1907–80 married
Otto Kohtes
1900–67
(no children)

(16)
Otto Lenneberg
1899–1944 married (5)
"Lina" Schneider
1894–1985

(16)
Otto Lenneberg
1899–1944

(5)
Franziska Karoline Scheider
1894–1985

Hans E. Pawel
1920–99

Ursula Lenneberg
1926–

Walter Lenneberg
1930–44

David J. Pawel
1955–
married Mayumi
Shibuya

Bruce R. Pawel
1958–
married Barbara
Slutsky

daughter:
Laura Elyse Pawel
1993–

MAP: My travels,

MILES
0   50   100   150   200

NORTH SEA

DENMARK

NETHERLANDS

Hamburg

Bremerhaven

Elbe

Bremen

GERMA

Münster

Lippborg

Warburg

Kassel

Oberkaufungen

Eschwege

Tennstedt

Kölleda

Dortmund

BELGIUM

Düsseldorf

Rhine

Straussfurt

Freyburg

Naumburg

Weissenfels

Borna

Rochlitz

Nuremberg

FRANCE

Danube

Munich

SWIZERLAND

JULY 1942–JUNE 1945

BALTIC SEA

Gdansk

Stettin

Present border

Hohenelbe

German border
before World War II

N Y

Berlin

POLAND

Trautenau

Landeshut

Mulde

Kölleda

Dresden

Reichenberg

Breslau

oder

Merzdorf

Liebau

Kattowitz

Cracow

Bodenbach

Tannenwald

Auschwitz

Theresienstadt

Prague

Kudowa-Sackisch

CZECH REPUBLIC

Moldau

Deggendorf

Present German Border
German Border before
  World War II
Author's journey

AUSTRIA

1 · The Family

I was born in 1926 in Dortmund, Germany. The renowned obstetrician who delivered me was a bit drunk, I was told, but my mother and I managed to survive the experience quite well. I had a very good early childhood, and even during the first two or three years of the Nazi era I still had a happy life, or as happy a life as any Jewish child could then enjoy in Germany. My parents raised me as a Jew; my father was Jewish and my mother came from a Christian family. When the Nazi persecution came, it caused me if anything to identify even more strongly as a Jew, although I had little religious influence from either of my parents.

The Nazi persecution was based on race. Racially I was a half-Jew (*ein Mischling*), but since I was given the Jewish religion I was considered a Jew and I always felt like a Jew. When all Jews had to add the middle name Sarah or Israel to their other names, and when all Jews had to wear the yellow *Magen David* (Star of David) on their outer clothing, it was natural for me to do so.

My mother and father met in Hagen, Westphalia, a medium-sized town in the northern part of western Germany, where they both worked as buyers at Leser's, a local department store.

My mother was born in 1894 in Dortmund. She completed an apprenticeship in merchandizing at Nassau's department store in Dortmund. She was one of the 11 children (of whom four died in infancy) of Joseph and Elisabeth Schneider. My maternal grandmother, Elisabeth Schneider, née Füllgraf, was born in 1868 in Grebenstein, a little village near Kassel. Her father had a woodworking shop, and he also played the fiddle. She was sent to Dortmund as a young woman to help an aunt who owned a grocery store there. One of the

1

customers she served was Joseph Schneider, my grandfather, who worked at the local utility plant as a plant engineer. He was Swiss, his journeyman wanderings having brought him to Dortmund. However, the Füllgrafs were Protestants, and he soon realized that he would never have a chance to marry Elisabeth Füllgraf because he was a Catholic, and therefore he kept it a secret all his life.

Nobody would have ever known his background if the Nazis had not demanded proof from his sons that the Schneider family was 100 per cent Aryan. It only came out because the confirmation they received from Zurich in 1938 also revealed that their father had been a Catholic. By that time my grandfather had died – but I am getting ahead of myself.

My father, Otto Lenneberg, was born in Düsseldorf in 1899. He was the youngest of the five children of Adolf and Amalie Lenneberg. Adolf Lenneberg and Amalie Bernard were distant cousins. The Lennebergs had been in Germany for generations. They were a totally assimilated Jewish family. I do not know when my Grandfather Lenneberg died – it may have been before I was born. One of his legs had been amputated, and I vaguely remember stories that the operation had been unnecessary. I do remember distinctly that his wooden leg stood in a closet, which was actually a corner of the bedroom with a curtain to conceal it. How shocked I was when I spotted it for the first time on one of my nosy sprees opening closets and cabinets.

My grandmother, Amalie Lenneberg – I called her 'Oma Lenneberg' – was probably born in 1868. She was of medium height and wore her grey hair bobbed, with a comb stuck either side of it. She usually wore black stockings and low-heeled black button shoes. Her dresses were loose-fitting, of black or grey material adorned with a brooch. She had very lively intelligent eyes. I never heard her raise her voice or show much emotion.

It was clear to everybody in the family that she was less than pleased when her youngest and favourite son Otto told her that he intended to marry Lina Schneider (her given name was Franziska Karoline). My grandmother did not want her son to marry a *Goyte* (a non-Jew). She was an intellectual snob, and considered herself superior in station and cultural background to the Schneiders. She also exhibited extreme distrust of my mother and her family. At that time her older son Erich was living with her and shared in the responsibility of running the business. He supported her objections to my father's marriage plans and he assured my grandmother that he could never cause her the kind of grief and suffering which my father was about to inflict upon her.

So it was that my parents married without the blessing of my father's parents at the home of my mother's parents in Dortmund in 1925. I was born about a year later, and I think my arrival softened Oma Lenneberg's resolve, and she even visited us in Aplerbeck. The relationship between her and my mother seemed just fine, although I am sure that their love for each other was barely skin-deep. I think both my mother and my father were particularly offended because it turned out that my Uncle Erich, while supporting my grandmother's objections to their marriage, and despite his own protestations of loyalty, had himself had a non-Jewish girlfriend for some time. When my uncle confronted his mother with the fact that he was going to marry her, Oma Lenneberg's reaction stunned everybody: she let her son Erich and Erna, his fiancée (said to be already pregnant at that point), share her house and, after their marriage, she allowed them to take over the management of the business.

I liked my Aunt Erna Lenneberg, Uncle Erich's new wife. She was a tall, thin woman with shiny, wavy black hair and a pretty, almost chiselled face. She was a devout Catholic and rarely missed Sunday Mass. It seemed to me that she was always carrying a big belly around with her. Aunt Erna obviously liked me too, as she named one of her daughters after me. All of Oma Lenneberg's love was devoted to my cousin Paul (son of Erich and Erna) and she practically raised him. None of the other grandchildren could compete with 'Paulchen' as she called him. My parents told me that Paul was duly circumcised and was given the Jewish religion at birth.

My Grandmother Lenneberg never went to synagogue,

but she did receive frequent visits from Rabbi Max Eschelbacher of the Reformed Düsseldorf Synagogue. He liked to talk to her as she was an interesting conversationalist and extremely well-read. Whenever he reminded her to attend services she assured him that if she wanted to talk to God she did not have to do so in the synagogue. She did not keep the Jewish holidays.

She told me once that the Lennebergs originally came from Spain, probably during the time of the Inquisition, then settled in Holland, and eventually some of them migrated into northwestern Germany and settled in a town called Lennep. The town is located on the River Lenne, not too far from Düsseldorf, and from that evolved the name Lenneberg.

My father's oldest brother, Walter, was killed as a German soldier at Verdun during World War I – a loss my grandmother felt keenly for the rest of her life. I understood that Uncle Erich was in fact her least favourite son, and that she had often criticized his character; but somehow, when her world came apart, she transferred all her love to his first son.

When I was a little girl, my father's oldest sister Erna Lenneberg-Meyer was my favourite aunt. Tante Erna (Aunt Erna) was born around 1895. She was on the short side, and she was endowed with a huge bosom. (It intrigued me that anybody could be appendaged with something so enormous.) She was intelligent and had strong opinions, which she did not hesitate to voice. Her husband Fritz Meyer had some type of engineering job. Both were good and loving people. They lived in a town called Mühlheim on the River Ruhr. They both adored me (they had no children of their own), and I liked all the attention they showered upon me.

Later, when they moved to Frankfurt am Main, I had many wonderful vacations with them. My aunt was a fastidious housekeeper and a good cook. She and I did a lot of baking together. What a mess I made! I got away with all the things I was not allowed to do at home. We went to the swimming club on the River Main. They took me to the circus, where we had a wonderful time. Uncle Fritz was a tall handsome man and he could make and fix anything. He mended their shoes and I watched him with utter fascination when he put new heels on my shoes. He was devoted to my aunt, and I never heard a cross word exchanged between them.

Aunt Else, my father's other sister, was married to Sally Hanauer, a merchant in Essen, Germany. They had two daughters, Ilse, the oldest, and Lotte, who was four years older than me. Tante (Aunt) Else and Onkel (Uncle) Sally had an unhappy marriage – stories were told in the family about his philandering ways. This atmosphere did not make for a happy home life for the girls. My cousin Lotte spent almost every vacation at our house, and she and I were close friends. We were very fond of each other.

Aunt Else was a good cook but a poor housekeeper. She was short and rotund, and wore her greying hair in a page-boy style. She had a very pretty, kind face and beautiful eyes and skin. She wore silk and rayon dresses, often spotted with cooking stains. She had a sweet disposition, and it was generally acknowledged that she was too nice a person, and therefore unable to cope with her husband's transgressions. I enjoyed the abundant supply of chocolates and cookies at her house. Sally Hanauer died during the early part of the Nazi years. His widow Else had limited resources, and as the Hitler persecution was getting progressively worse, work opportunities for Jews became impossible to find. Eventually, she and her oldest daughter Ilse had to take jobs keeping house for wealthy Jewish widowers. I visited them with my parents and my brother, each in her new milieu – a milieu which my father found quite disturbing. I also remember my father's unsuccessful efforts to persuade Herr Samuel, Aunt Else's employer, to marry her.*

I always felt very close to my mother's family. I loved my Grandmother Schneider. I am still convinced that there has never been a more wonderful grandmother than 'Oma' (as I called her). She was a petite grey-haired woman, with beautiful grey-green eyes and unblemished smooth skin. She had frameless glasses, and wore her long hair away from her

---

*Aunt Else died in Stutthof (concentration camp) in December 1944. Ilse Hanauer perished in a Polish camp. A children's transport took Lotte to Palestine. She now lives in Germany.

face. She braided her hair and knotted it into a bun, taking great care to wave the front of it above her forehead with a waving iron which she heated on a small dry spirit-burner. She was a fastidious dresser. Although most of her dresses were black or patterned on black or grey backgrounds, she often wore white starched collars and cuffs, or lace-adorned collars held in place with her favourite brooch. She wore black or grey stockings and low-heeled leather lace-up shoes. She would rarely go shopping without a hat. She was a very energetic lady and could get quite upset when she disapproved of something. She was open in her dealings with people and she expected everybody else to be the same.

As a little girl I hated to be bathed, but I loved it when Oma washed me. She had the right touch. She was gentle, always reassuring. She used to put a very large basin on a wooden bench in the kitchen and fill it with warm water, making sure that the temperature was just right. I stood on a little stool, and she would wash me, one area at a time, from top to toe. She was usually outraged that '*das arme Kind*' (the poor child) had not been washed properly in weeks, since my ears and toes were not cleaned to her liking.

My grandparents Schneider lived in a first-floor apartment on Olga Strasse, No. 15, in Dortmund. Olga Strasse was a very nice street with well-kept private homes and small apartment houses. Each house had a small front lawn with plants and flowers protected by a heavy ornate iron fence. No. 15 also had a nice tree-shaded backyard. The entrance hall of the four-family building was beautifully tiled, the wood trim and stair-railings were of heavily carved oak, the brass trim on the doors was polished to a high gloss. The apartment had a long narrow entrance hall with an oak wardrobe and mirror. Of course, there was a fairly large all-important kitchen which was furnished with a comfortable large sofa, a big table with an inlaid linoleum top, chairs and huge kitchen cabinets which were actually pieces of furniture. The oversized, coal-fired cooking stove was polished to perfection and the big sink was equipped only with a cold-water tap. The kitchen was a bright, cheerful place with a huge window overlooking the lovely garden which contained an oval flower-bed that my grandmother tended with her usual love and devotion.

The pantry was directly off the kitchen, with an ice box instead of a refrigerator to keep stored foods cold in the warm season. The ice was bought in the street in large blocks from the horse-drawn wagon of the ice man. The clatter of the wagon wheels and his shouts of 'ice, ice, ice!' could be heard through the whole neighbourhood.

Family life centred around the kitchen where all meals were served; the formal dining room was used only on holidays or to receive important visitors. It was furnished with large, heavy pieces of dark-stained oak furniture. I was fascinated with the Victrola (gramophone) with its crooked arm which my aunt had to swing around to make it play. There was a large picture over the sideboard which, as my grandmother explained to me, depicted the 'Alten Fritz' (Frederick the Great) being entertained in one of the great halls at Sans-Souci. Oma had enormously large potted plants on every windowsill. Some, called clivias, had magnificent red blossoms.

The apartment had huge windows and since it was located on the first floor my grandfather was very much afraid of burglars. Whenever they went away for any length of time, even just for a whole day, he would put large wooden shutters against the inside of the windows; they were held in place by two large iron bars which fitted crosswise into brackets. This ritual fascinated me – there was some of the cops-and-robbers spookiness about it.

I would often accompany my grandmother when she went into the basement where she stored coal, potatoes, onions, apples, sauerkraut and french-cut stringbeans preserved in large earthenware jars; jams and fruit and vegetables were conserved in glass jars. Before we would venture into the basement she would light the wick of the oil lamp and then replace the cylinder over it, and I would then help her to bring up the stored foods or the coal for the kitchen stove. The house had electricity, but there was none in the basement. They had no central heating system: their only source of heat was the kitchen stove. The huge tiled stove in the living room was only used on holidays. The bedrooms were, of course, unheated and they would be bitterly cold in the winter. The toilet too could get very cold, so the chamber-pot was a welcome solution.

One day Oma Schneider was cleaning some storage space, and she came upon a trunk which was filled to the brim with money bills in huge denominations. As she was holding up a 100,000 Reichsmark note, she explained that it would not have bought a loaf of bread during the terrible inflation after World War I. 'Urselchen those were bad times! There was violence – many people were out of work.'

I liked going shopping with my grandmother. We would walk to the farmer's market with two large shopping bags and two additional bags made of netting. She inspected every fruit and vegetable and she always bought something which I liked very much like *Zwieback* covered with chocolate frosting or almond paste at Fischer's bakery.

She treasured a postcard which her oldest son Heinrich had sent her from France as a German soldier in World War I. It was a photograph taken in the trenches of a mock wedding scene with my Uncle Heinrich dressed up as the bride. The postcard immediately struck my grandmother as a bad omen. Soon after, my Uncle Heinrich was killed. She mourned all her life for her son and for her little daughter Erna who died of diphtheria when she was three years old. Little 'Ernachen', as she would refer to her, was buried in a cemetery about half an hour's walk from her house. She would visit her grave about once a week, and she took great care to plant flowers, rake the soil and then just quietly reflect. This was something we did together so often that I almost felt I knew the little girl.

My grandfather Joseph Schneider was born in 1866 in Zurich, Switzerland. He was a handsome man, who took great care of his appearance. He was at least six foot tall. He had a full head of greying hair which had been jet black when he was a young man. He had an olive complexion, a small, well-trimmed moustache and round glasses resting on his long straight nose. He usually wore a three-piece suit. His golden pocket-watch was on a long gold chain which was threaded through one of the buttonholes of his jacket. His shoes always shone to perfection.

I loved my 'Opa' Schneider, and would have never believed that he had any faults, but I was to learn many years later that he did indeed have some weaknesses after all. After work, Opa Schneider liked his schnapps, and he frequented a tavern which was located near his place of work. This was a great source of grief and pain for my grandmother, who had to put up with a husband who drank while she was constantly pregnant. He also occasionally liked other women. At least once my oldest uncle, Willi, and my mother literally dragged him out of the apartment of a woman he was in the habit of seeing. An interested party had made sure to feed this information back to my grandmother. He was quite drunk at the time of the incident. My mother threatened the 'lady' quite successfully, and this episode came to an abrupt conclusion.

Opa Schneider never lost his Swiss accent, and he used to call me '*Puppele*' (Swiss-German for little doll). He patiently played games with me, especially card games like 'Schwarzer Peter', which I loved and I suspect that he, at least occasionally, let me win. He would yodel for me and I begged him to do it again and again, until the poor man was hoarse. At seventy-one he became bedridden with cancer. He was so ill and weak, and I was overwhelmed by the changes in him. My grandmother tended to him day and night. Everybody seemed so sad and subdued. I sensed that something terrible was taking place – and then he died, either in 1937 or 1938.

As far back as I can remember I always loved my mother's oldest sister Tante Minchen (Aunt Minchen). Aunt Minchen was born in 1892. She was short, with brown curly hair, and she wore thick glasses to correct her extreme near-sightedness. She was in the habit of talking rapidly and never finishing her sentences. She was a clean, hardworking person, and selfless and generous to a fault. When I was a little girl Aunt Minchen was the manager of a bakery branch store in a small town near the city of Dortmund. I was happy when she found employment as a bookkeeper in a bank in Dortmund. This gave her more free time and I was to benefit from that very often. There was nothing more exciting for me than to go to a fair or circus with Tante Minchen. We would return home laden with teddy bears, balloons, enormous cheap dolls, messy candy – everything wonderful! My aunt's reception from her younger sister Mille was less enthusiastic than I thought she and I deserved. She found it incomprehensible that anybody would squander money on such junk. The words 'You have no sense at all!' still ring in my ears.

I liked Tante Mille, and I know that she really loved me in her own way, but she was easily offended and I thought her too stingy. She would not do the things with me that I considered fun, and she lacked the goodnatured disposition of my Aunt Minchen. My grandmother blamed herself for the shortcomings of her youngest daughter. She told my mother many times: 'I cried for nine months, I did not want any more children. I was so miserable, I am sure it had an effect on her!'

I spent a lot of time at my grandparents' home when I was a little girl. At that time Aunt Mille was a woman in her early twenties. She was quite pretty with a petite figure, jet-black wavy hair and unblemished skin and beautiful teeth. She had a passion for stylish clothes. Aunt Mille was much younger than any of her brothers and sisters, and as sometimes happens to the last-born, her parents spoiled her. She did most of the cleaning and household chores in their home, but she never held an outside job. Perhaps because of this her interests were somewhat limited.

My grandmother did send her to a cookery school where she learned to make confections, fancy biscuits and cakes which she stored in colourful metal tins. If she wanted to have anything left for the holidays she had to hide it from my Uncle Konrad, who was still living at home, and from me, but we were very good at discovering her secret places. We toasted rye bread directly on the hot metal stove top and then covered it with lots of butter. The kitchen was filled with the scrumptious aroma of toasted bread. We messed up her shining stove top and we usually got hell for it, but it was all worth it.

There were frequent confrontations between my grandfather and his youngest daughter Mille. She ran the household and often alienated her brothers and sisters – they even accused her of driving them away from their parents' home. Certainly no one could have suggested that she did this to my father on whom she had a terrible crush.

One Easter weekend we came to Dortmund to visit my grandparents. We found the entire Schneider family assembled there in a state of tension and dismay because my Aunt Mille had decided to strip the paint off the kitchen cabinets which were lined up on the lawn in the garden, where she was in the process of revarnishing them. I don't know if my grandmother was more concerned about the upheaval in her house or the dreadful thought: 'What are people going to say, when they see you doing this on Easter Sunday?' My mother was outraged, but there was never much point in arguing with Aunt Mille.

My Uncle Konrad was born in 1905. He was a handsome young man with a dashing appearance. Women were crazy about him. An unfortunate result was that at one time he had a brief affair with a married woman at least 15 years his senior. What made it particularly bad was that this lady's husband was a friend of his, and that they had a seven-year-old boy. Once I visited them with my uncle at their apartment. His ladyfriend opened the door in her slip, and my uncle greeted her with a friendly slap on her ample behind. I am sorry to confess that I faithfully reported this when I returned to my grandmother's house. All the same Uncle Konrad was my favourite uncle. I knew that he loved me, and he and I always had some conspiracy going.

Uncle Konrad married a lovely young woman. Everybody liked her although there were some remarks about her family's Polish background. They had no children. (It must be a statistical oddity that of my grandmother's 11 children, only five survived, and of them only my mother was able to have children.)

Uncle Konrad and Uncle Willi worked for the Electric Company like my grandfather. Uncle Konrad was an electrical technician, and Uncle Willi was an electrical engineer. It was very difficult to obtain secure jobs in Germany in the late 1920s, but my grandfather had done extremely well in providing for his two sons.

Uncle Willi had some of my grandfather's good looks but he was not as handsome as his younger brother. He was capable and ambitious and successful as an engineer with the power company. He was nice to me when I was very small, but I never felt the warmth and love from him that had developed into a bond between Uncle Konrad and myself. He was married to Luzi Eisel, a good-looking blonde, with a pleasingly plump figure and an infectious, vulgar laugh. My grandmother was not totally taken with her daughter-in-law. I liked Tante Luzi, and I visited their lovely apartment many times, but our families were never very close.

2 • My Early Life

In 1925 my father became general manager of the Karstadt department store in Aplerbeck, and my mother became buyer for children's and ladies' clothing there. The store was part of a chain which owned and operated department stores throughout Germany. At that time Aplerbeck (located near the city of Dortmund in Westphalia, in the western part of Germany) was a small town.

My parents were newly weds and lived in a beautiful, very large apartment on the top floor of the multi-storey department store building. This was sheer luxury: four bedrooms, two baths, a toilet, living room, dining room, study, parlour, kitchen and pantries and playroom. The rooms were beautifully furnished with oriental rugs and lovely paintings, figurines and vases made of fine china, elegant curtains, mahogany and fruitwood furniture and large tiled fireplaces.

My father's study was lined with books. The centrepiece of the room was a huge desk with a chair upholstered in leather. A large bookcase occupied one entire wall. His study was off-limits to me but I liked to browse around and sit in the huge chair when nobody was around to reprimand me.

I had all this to myself until 23 September 1930, when my brother Walter was born. I cannot remember whether I was glad to have a new baby in the house, but the intrusion of Schwester Berna, the baby-nurse, who became a member of the household, was something I just had to put up with.

I felt that she disturbed my day-dreaming and ruined my privacy. There was a very small toilet at the end of the apartment. A large heating pipe protruded through the floor and connected to the steampipes which fed the rest of the rooms. It was remote and very private since nobody used it. It was an especially snug place in the autumn and winter where

I spent hours day-dreaming and fantasizing. I was occasionally asked: 'Where have you been, we have been looking for you for hours?' I was determined not to give my secret away. Unfortunately, my hiding place was discovered and I was nicknamed *'Träumlieschen'* (little dreamer). I was convinced that Schwester Berna had spied on me. Sometime later my mother felt it necessary to discharge her.

Grete was our maid of all work. She had a sunny disposition, was efficient, and I liked her a lot. She was a young local woman in her early twenties of simple background. She especially liked my father, who was always very kind and never demanding. One could not say the same of my mother, who accused my father of giving everybody a chance to take advantage of him, and I think she was right about this, as some of their later experiences clearly proved. Grete had an unfortunate accident when she cut herself while opening a can, and then paid no further attention to it. A horrible infection developed, and for many weeks I sat next to her on my little footstool while she was bathing her hand in soapy water. My father took care of her treatment and made her bathe it every hour – these were the days before penicillin. Grete was unable to do housework for a very long time. Everybody was relieved when the wound finally showed signs of healing.

My parents were grateful that my Aunt Mille (my mother's youngest sister) joined our household when Grete became incapacitated. As usual my father and Aunt Mille got along well, but my mother complained that she had to treat her with kid gloves. I think Aunt Mille always felt inferior to my mother: she wanted to make sure that my mother did not think of her as an employee or a servant. She must have resented running the household, while my mother, well dressed and successful, went about her business managing her department and her personnel. My parents were very generous to Aunt Mille. She frequently joined us on vacation and they showered her with gifts.

My cousin Lotte Hanauer spent a lot of time at our house. We loved each other like sisters. Lotte was about four years older than me. We liked to play shops. (I guess our surroundings had some influence on us.) One Christmas we were presented with a little shop, which my father had designed and built with the assistance of the department store's caretaker and handyman, Jupp Geschwind. The shop consisted of front and back walls which were 5 feet tall and 6 feet wide, these were held together with arches on both sides. It contained uncountable drawers with labels, glass show cases, large candy jars, a scale with weights, paper bags and shovels. A cash register with real paper money and coins, bills and pencils, miniature boxes of oatmeal, cocoa, flour, salt, sugar – the works. The shop was a delight. We were busy selling from morning to night, and my Grandfather Schneider must have gone broke during that Christmas vacation. One day Lotte and I got into a very silly mood and ate all the sweets and chocolates in our store, thereby breaking a solemn promise we had given. We received a severe dressing down and our stomachs didn't feel too good either.

Another favourite toy of mine was a beautiful life-size celluloid doll. It was as large as an 18-month baby boy. He had movable limbs and eyes, and he would say 'Mama' when I turned him on his stomach. His name was Hans. I don't know why I chose that name. Hans had a huge wardrobe so Lotte and I were kept busy dressing him and taking him for walks in a beautiful baby carriage.

There was a large cobblestone courtyard at the back of the department store building. At the end of the yard were numerous storage buildings and covered work areas which were mostly used for packing and unpacking merchandise. I loved to play house in huge cartons and crates and specially in areas which were off-limits to me. I was scolded when I was caught because my father considered these places unsafe for me. My protector and accomplice was Jupp Geschwind. Jupp was so ugly that he fascinated me. He was very short, he had small piercing eyes, and an unusually large nose, and about two teeth left in his upper and lower jaws. He wore frayed clothing and always old, dirty high boots. He lived on the outskirts of the town, in the rural, impoverished countryside, in a small house which he had built himself, and which resembled a large crate covered with the tarpaper used in building to cover roofs. He had a wife, a pig and chickens. He taught me how to ride a bicycle which was much too big for me, and during his lunch-break we would often bicycle to his house. This was a wonderful adventure for me. I liked Jupp, he could fix anything and his family always made a fuss of me. I liked the pig and her piglets, and it did not bother me that the house was very untidy. They did their own butchering and I enjoyed everything they offered me to eat. My parents were very generous to the Geschwinds, but I thought them to be quite unreasonable when they questioned me about my frequent visits there, and I resented their obvious disapproval.

For my birthday in 1932 I received a beautiful brand new bike with large balloon tyres and all the shining accessories to go with it. My father, my cousin Lotte and I enjoyed wonderful bicycle trips through the woods and surrounding hills and valleys. We usually stopped at an inn for refreshments. The innkeeper knew my father and we always received a warm welcome. Every effort to teach my mother to ride a bicycle failed miserably. As soon as she realized that my father was not holding on to the back of her carrier anymore, she would panic, and she would ultimately fall off the bike, accusing my father: 'You let me fall!' (*Du hast mich fallen lassen!*).

In 1932 I started school (*Volksschule*) in Aplerbeck. On the first day of school it was customary to receive a large cardboard container shaped like a horn which was covered with fancy, colourful paper, decorations and bows, and filled to the brim with all kinds of sweets and goodies. It was known as a *Schultüte*, and I received a beautiful one. I proudly posed for pictures with two little girls who were my playmates: one the daughter of a local physician and the other the daughter of the head of the local school.

Grandmother Schneider's stories about the farm area around Grebenstein, the village where she was born, aroused enough interest in my father to take me there during the summer vacation. We stayed on a farm and I vaguely remember the cobblestone streets, the horse-drawn wagons and the smell of dung. We arrived there by train and I treasured the two train tickets which the conductor had given to me. A little girl who was playing in the street wanted one of my tickets but I refused to let her have it. To punish my selfishness my father made me give it to her. I did so without acknowledging her existence, convinced that I had suffered a great injustice. I spent several summer vacations in Grebenstein, living on the farm and enjoying milk, butter and cheese from natural, good 'wholesome' (unpasteurized!) milk. My mother had also spent many vacations on the same farm as a little girl.

In 1933, after I had started first grade at school, I complained of a painful swelling on the right side of my neck. I had a very swollen, pulsating lymph gland filled with pus. After many visits to doctors, including consultations with specialists from Düsseldorf to Berlin, a diagnosis of scrofula (tuberculosis of the lymph glands from unpasteurized milk) was made. I was treated with applications of some substance out of a can, which was heated and then applied to my gland to draw out the pus. My gland was tender and painful, and I screamed every time they applied it even before it touched my skin. The gland drained for a very long time, it would open, close up again, and finally had to be lanced. One specialist used a huge syringe with an enormous needle to extract the pus. My neck was bandaged for more than a year. My mother experienced the same infection as a child, but she was treated by an old country physician who made a large clean cut to drain her lymph gland. She was not left with multiple calcified nodules in her neck which I have had ever since. Nobody ever associated her problem with ingesting milk from cows infected with tuberculosis. It was only years later that a radiologist in Düsseldorf solved the mystery.

Whenever my father returned from a business trip he came home with a surprise, but the sudden appearance of 'Böbchen', a very cute, tiny black Dachshund puppy was very special. It also caused a lot of commotion since he preferred to do his business on our oriental rugs. I wanted to play with him but he was very scared and elusive. He was so shy that he tried to hide in the most unlikely places. We all tried to track him down because my mother had threatened to get rid of him if he went on soiling her precious rugs. She won out over our objections, and sadly he had to go to a kind relative (who also pronounced him untrainable after a supposedly fair chance).

3 · *The Nazi Era Begins*

Our life changed on 30 January 1933, when Hitler became Chancellor of Germany and immediately put his ideas into effect – particularly his restrictions on large Jewish-owned businesses. The Nazis spread anti-Jewish propaganda and any useless hoodlum had the chance to see himself in a brown or black uniform. *En masse* these criminals followed the orders of Hitler's henchmen with enthusiasm.

The Karstadt department store which my father managed was owned and operated by a German-Jewish concern. It was one of the first major business organizations forced to sell out to 'Aryan' management (*Arisierung*). All Jews connected with the corporation were forced to leave their jobs immediately.

The word 'boycott' suddenly had a very personal meaning for us. Uniformed Nazi thugs were positioned in front of Jewish-owned stores and they dared customers to enter them. They then proceeded to arrest Jewish men at random. Some were released promptly, while others had their first taste of prison. The audacity and the cruelty of these 'SA-*Männer*', the Brownshirts, who wore high leather boots and swastika armbands, and their brethren in black shirts who belonged to the SS, were impossible for sane people to comprehend.

Most of these rogues had never been able to hold down a job, and some of them were former convicts and even murderers. They seized the opportunity to belong: their newly found power made them feel important and feared. Now they were part of a horde and they were capable of immense savagery. These were the people who confiscated Jewish properties and businesses. They profited directly from their criminal activities and convinced themselves and others that Germany's 525,000 Jews – roughly 1 per cent of the German population – were to blame for their and all of Germany's problems, and whatever they seized was due them because they were the real Germans who had been wronged.

The Rosensteins, owners of a featherbedding store in Aplerbeck, had been good friends of my parents for many years. In the spring of 1933 the Rosensteins urged my parents to leave Germany, but unfortunately they brushed these warnings aside. Even now, I can still almost hear their oft-repeated phrase about Hitler: 'The thug won't be in power for long' (*Der Verbrecher bleibt nicht dran*).

My father bought a large store almost next door to the department store he had been forced to leave. He purchased the hardware, houseware and porcelain, crystal and glassware store from the Steinweg family who were leaving Germany. In spite of the bad political climate, the store flourished.

The parents of my best playmates, the children who had posed with me for the photo of our first day of school in 1932, now barely one year later no longer allowed them to play or even associate with me. It was impossible for me, a seven-year-old, to understand when one after another of my 'friends' told me: 'I cannot play with you any more because you are Jewish!'

In 1934 I was forced to leave the school in Aplerbeck, and I entered the *Jüdische Volksschule* (Jewish elementary school) in Dortmund. I had to travel by tram from Aplerbeck to Dortmund for about 30 minutes each way. I had missed almost one year of school because of the scrofula, so to make up for the lost time, my father found a tutor for me. She was a retired teacher, Frau Buchheim, the wife of the principal of the Jewish school, and she agreed to tutor me every day after school at my Grandmother Schneider's house in Dortmund. She was in her late forties, a good-looking, smartly dressed woman with a personality which demanded instant respect. Frau Buchheim had made arrangements with my father for his secretary, Fräulein Schlecht, to supervise my studies and homework which she assigned at every session. Fräulein Schlecht was a tall, thin, middle-aged woman. She wore her hair pulled back into a bun, her dress was very conservative, almost severe, and her manners were a bit old-maidish and provincial. She was convinced from the start that she would be qualified to tutor me herself and she resented Frau Buchheim, even though she had never met her.

Since my total interest was not always with my studies, I often did not satisfy either lady, but with their help, unbeknown to them, I got the better of them by playing one off against the other and thereby deflecting all criticism. When Fräulein Schlecht found fault with Frau Buchheim's method I gleefully related her remarks to Frau Buchheim and vice versa. I must have relished every minute of it since I kept adding more spice to the dispute, even inventing a few extra remarks. This innocent little game mushroomed into a real crisis between the two ladies with harsh letter exchanges and accusations. I stood by innocently until my father discovered the source of it all. I was made to feel very naughty and guilty, and I have never forgotten this incident of intrigue of which I was the central character.

My Grandmother Schneider was horrified and incredulous since I got her involved as well. She just could not comprehend that her 'Urselchen' could fabricate lies and weave intrigues. Her calm but utterly shattered reactions made an enormous impression on me, and I vowed to myself not to do anything like it again.

When I started school in Dortmund I was assigned a seat in the last row of my classroom. I was quite near-sighted, a fact which my parents were unaware of, and I made up for it by guessing since I could not read the blackboard. The statistics worked against me in this guessing game, and I turned out to be the least bright child in the class. The teacher was convinced that I was a hopeless case.

Our maid Grete did not believe this since I had been able to read children's books as well as the labels of sugar, flour, coffee, tea and more on the many porcelain jars on the top shelves of the kitchen cupboards. Unbeknown to me she had recently dusted those shelves and when she replaced the jars, she had inadvertently mixed them up. Convinced that the teachers at the school in Dortmund did not know their business, she asked me to read the descriptions on the jars.

Unaware of the mix up, I read, rather quoted from memory according to the old line-up of the jars with total self-confidence. So Grete made the diagnosis: 'Ursel does not read, she guesses, maybe she has a problem with her eyes?' The ophthalmologist in Dortmund concurred with the findings of myopia and astigmatism and prescribed my first pair of glasses, which I hated.

I sensed that my parents were upset and I decided that these dark horn-rimmed glasses made me look ugly. I had to admit to myself that the world looked a lot brighter, but I still tried not to wear them, particularly since some of the boys in my class called me 'bespectacled snake' (*Brillenschlange* – the German word for cobra). After some time had elapsed the glasses became part of me, the world looked too dull and faint without them.

The Kahns, old friends of my parents, had a men's clothing store on the main street where most of the businesses were located. They had no children but a huge German shepherd dog called Argo who lived in a kennel on a very long chain. I was a frequent visitor at their house. One nice summer day I was swinging in their hammock, as I had done so very often, when my buttocks in the swinging hammock came close enough to Argo's teeth, and to my horror and surprise he bit me. That was undoubtedly the day when I started to mistrust and fear German shepherds. I have always liked all kinds of animals, especially dogs, but unfortunately the German shepherd became a symbol of evil to me – even today I am not totally free of this prejudice.

The Wissbrunns, also friends of my parents, had a shoe shop next door to us. They owned the building and lived in a very spacious apartment above the store. I was fascinated by the machine into which I could stick my feet with the new shoes on them, and Mr Wissbrunn would assure my mother that the X-ray image convinced him that I was perfectly fitted. (This wonderful machine had a real fluoroscopic X-ray screen. I just hope that my mother did not buy too many pairs of new shoes for me from Sally Wissbrunn!)

Some of my father's friends played a card game called Skaat. My father was not a card-player, and therefore was not able to join their group. The chief organizer was Sally Wissbrunn, who at one time was also in charge of a big dinner party for their club. In spite of urgings from the other members, he refused to invite my father to the feast, because to him a refusal to play Skaat was sacrilegious. The others kept my father informed about the details and preparations including a prized roast goose personally prepared by Frau Wissbrunn, who was referred to in our house as *'Röllchen'* (little roll) because of her ample circumference.

My father did not take this lying down and plotted his revenge with the help, and to the delight, of some of the other card-players. He asked his secretary, Fräulein Schlecht, to call Frau Wissbrunn and to keep her on the phone as long as possible. While Fräulein Schlecht was on the phone with Frau Wissbrunn, our janitor and my father erected a ladder to the Wissbrunn's kitchen window. The telephone was located in the hall so that the kitchen was all clear for the quick removal of the beautifully roasted goose in its heavy cast-iron pan. This horrible deed was accomplished through the upper-storey kitchen window. The ensuing scandal branded my father as the *'Gänsedieb'* (the thief who stole the goose).

After the Nazi coup in 1933 restrictions, boycotts and persecution of Jews were getting worse week by week and month by month. It became very difficult for non-Jews to work in Jewish businesses. These people found themselves intimidated and threatened by the Brownshirts, and often by their own families who felt that they were being endangered themselves. As a result my father lost a large number of his employees.

I was very sad when our maid Grete also left us. She had been with us as long as I could remember. It became too dangerous for her, and especially for my father, to have a gentile maid living in a Jewish home. The Nüremberg edicts (*Nurnberger Gesetze*)* forbade any sexual contact between Jews and gentiles, and Jewish men were many times falsely charged with having affairs with gentile women. These

---

*These edicts withdrew German citizenship from persons of 'non-German blood' in late 1935. They were particularly directed against Jews.

accusations often resulted in severe punishment, prison and sometimes death. My Aunt Minchen, my mother's oldest sister, left her bank job in Dortmund and decided to work for my parents in our store. My Aunt Mille was a frequent visitor as well, and she often lent a hand in the house.

Even though my parents tried to shield their children as much as they could I was terribly frightened when I saw and heard the crashing noise as our and our Jewish neighbour's store windows were repeatedly smashed by club-wielding Brownshirts. I did not understand why this was happening, but I sensed from the expression on my parents' and my aunts' faces that something horrible was going on. In town 'JEWS NOT WELCOME' signs appeared in some stores, on buildings, cultural institutions, theatres and cinemas. Our store was boycotted more frequently now, and 'DON'T BUY FROM THE JEW' signs were posted on Jewish shop windows. Some of my father's old customers who wanted to continue buying from him felt intimidated by the uniformed SA-*Männer* posted at the entrance of the store, twirling their truncheons and shouting threats at anybody who wanted to enter.

Since Aplerbeck was a small town with few Jewish families it became impossible to continue living there, and it also became clear that my parents had to sell the store. They did so in 1936. They found a German Catholic buyer, a decent man, who paid my parents a fair price for the store. (Such fair and honest behaviour was very unusual in those times.)

Shortly before we left Aplerbeck I visited my grandparents. My Grandmother Schneider had just returned from Sunday services at the Reinoldi Kirche, an imposing, large Protestant church in Dortmund. She was so terribly upset, she was crying and inconsolable. When she finally calmed down, she related that during his sermon, her favourite minister had severely criticized the Nazis. He had given a stinging rebuke to the 'thugs who are persecuting and harming our Jewish citizens'. He had not yet finished his sermon when uniformed Nazis stormed the pulpit and arrested him. Many years later I was told that he was never heard of again.

4 · Düsseldorf

My parents decided to move to Düsseldorf in 1936. (My father was born there and his mother, brother and cousins all lived there.) Düsseldorf was a large city with international visitors and businesses, a good-sized Jewish community and an excellent private Jewish school, which they felt would provide a safety net for them. My grandmother owned a beautiful store on Friedrichstrasse, which was one of the premier business streets in the city. My grandfather started the store, probably some 40 years earlier, when he was a young man. They sold the finest porcelain and crystal, statues, delicate Dresden dolls, animals and figurines. Of course, everything was off-limits to me and my brother. My grandmother owned and lived in the building above the store.

Our first apartment on Kirchfeldstrasse in Düsseldorf was very nice and spacious. Kirchfeldstrasse was a tree-lined street in a good neighbourhood, centrally located and not too far from my grandmother's house. We immediately started school at the private Jewish school (*Privat Jüdische Schule*) on Kasernenstrasse. I cannot recollect much about life on Kirchfeldstrasse, except that the apartment was nicely decorated with the remaining furniture, rugs and pictures which we had brought from Aplerbeck. (Before our move, my parents had sold many of their possessions, at bargain prices, mostly to newly rich Nazis.)

My father needed additional capital since he was planning to open another store in Düsseldorf. He started a wholesale dry goods business which included soap, perfume and beauty products. His customers were pedlars and gypsies. In spite of all the adversities the store was a huge success. It was located on Karlstrasse near the railway station.

Karlstrasse had always been the wholesale district but it was also the red-light district of the city. A few of my parents' pedlar customers were 'solid' German ladies who sympathized with our plight. I remember one in particular who was quite successful trading in pine-scented bath salts. She was a shrewd operator with a huge black-market business on the side. She supplied my mother with meat and other foods. She was a woman of simple background with a commanding presence, 'with her heart in the right place', as my mother put it so very often.

My mother did not trust the gypsies. I remember an incident when two gypsy women wanted to buy some merchandise. My mother whispered to me to watch one of them while she attended to the other. The woman finally confronted me and said in broken German: 'Have no fear – we don't steal!' I felt so guilty but I still did not trust her.

The two apartments above our store were the living quarters of ladies of the night with their 'husbands' as I was made to believe, but in reality their men were their pimps. A number of the adjacent houses were inhabited by ladies of the same profession. It was a relatively good atmosphere because these people were more friendly and sympathetic to us than the 'respectable' Germans. I was too young to know about such things, but I sometimes wondered about their dress, make-up and high heels. I also could not understand why they were constantly walking up and down the pavement. I only learned about their profession many years later.

We had to move again as the apartment on Kirchfeldstrasse had to be vacated for more privileged (non-Jewish) tenants. So we moved into my grandmother's house on Friedrichstrasse. An apartment in her house had become vacant because the tenant, who had lived there for many years, announced that she was not going to live in a 'Jew house' any longer. Before she left her apartment, she poisoned my grandmother's cat Illy.

My Grandmother Lenneberg was running the store with her son Erich. Erich's wife Erna was (as I have mentioned) a devout Catholic, and the Erich Lennebergs even in the worst of times of Nazi persecution obviously did not believe in birth control. Their oldest son Paul was born when Hitler came to power; subsequently they had three more children, Ursel, Mädi and Peter. Paul, who was called Paulchen was, according to a number of family members, given the Jewish religion at birth which was recorded in the register of the Jewish community in Düsseldorf (*Jüdische Kultusgemeinde*). The very same records contained the names of my brother and myself, and were later used by the Gestapo to designate children of mixed marriages as either Jewish or of (preferential) mixed-race status (*Priviligierte Mischlinge*).

The designation of a half-Jew who had been given the Jewish religion at birth was 'Jewish Individual of Mixed Race' (*Mischling*). A half-Jew who had been given the Christian religion at birth was 'Individual of Preferential Mixed-Race Status' (*Priviligierter Mischling*). Generally, a half-Jew of preferential mixed-race status was spared many of the restrictions imposed on half-Jews raised in the Jewish religion. There came a time when Jews and half-Jews of the Jewish faith were not permitted to convert to a Christian religion anymore.

It seemed that every street corner had a three-walled open kiosk showing a large display of the Nazis' most infamous propaganda tabloid, Julius Streicher's *Der Stürmer* (a *Stürmer* is a fighter who takes the enemy by storm). These vicious sheets showed caricatures of Jews with eye-catching captions and drawings. Jews were depicted as the source of all the evil that had ever befallen pure Aryan Germans and Germany: as fat, ugly money-changers who indulged in the spilling of Christian blood as part of their sinister customs and religious rites. I would walk by and catch a glimpse of this vile, but at the same time fascinating, display. If I felt unobserved, I would actually stop and look at these caricatures and read the hateful captions which described us.

The noose was being tightened more and more. My grandmother and Uncle Erich were forced to sell the store to Nazis from Munich for a ridiculously small sum of money. Since they had to vacate the entire building within a very short time, they sold their entire inventory for next to nothing because the buyers were not interested in porcelain and crystal. (The Münchs wanted the building and the location to open their linen and fancy bedding store.) Of course, they also demanded our apartment, and we had to move yet again. Each move was to more primitive quarters. My parents sold more furniture, paintings and rugs. My father was forced to sell his wholesale business on Karlstrasse since Jews could no longer own businesses; nor could they be employed.

My mother tried to find a job as a buyer in a large department store. She travelled to Berlin where she tried to make use of her old connections. I remember how carefully she dressed, using accessories to look chic. She had to get a job as she was now the sole breadwinner. Most of mother's business friends had been Jewish and they were all gone. When she arrived in Berlin, her non-Jewish former friends gave her a very cool reception, but she eventually found a position in Düsseldorf as a forelady in a leather-belt factory. This factory was owned by the family Schreyeck, a decent devout Catholic family who totally disapproved of the Nazis.

Since my father was now unemployed, Mr Schreyeck suggested that my mother take some work home. This enabled my father to earn some money gluing leather-belts and covering buckles with leather, hammering leather straps to wooden clogs and whatever other piece-work was available. Of course, he was not officially on their payroll.

5 · Lippborg

I remember my last vacation in Lippborg at my Aunt Minchen's, although I am not sure whether it was the summer of 1938 or 1939. My Uncle Franz, my Aunt Minchen's husband, was a member of the Brownshirts, the SA. SA stood for *Sturmabteilung* (Storm Detachment), a paramilitary Nazi force. He made my aunt join the Nazi Women's Auxiliary (*Frauenschaft*), which at first she strenuously objected to but then changed her mind. She told me, 'When I send those baskets of food and whatever else I can do to help your Mami and Papi and Bübchen and you, I am more effective when I wear the swastika button [*Hakenkreuz*]; then nobody questions my motives!' In fact she only wore the 'damned thing' (as she called and cursed it) to effect her goal of helping us.

On my last visit there she took me to a large gathering – a festival which she had to attend. Everybody stood to sing the Nazi song '*Die Fahne Hoch*' (Hold the Flag High) with their arms raised in the Hitler salute. She winked at me and encouraged me to follow her example, which I did, pretending to sing along. This charade served the purpose to keep herself above suspicion so that she could continue to help us, and she managed that brilliantly. Aunt Minchen might not have been the brightest, most sophisticated woman, but she used enormous common sense, her priority was always clear: she was unwavering in her support of us even though she was endangering herself.

My aunt's life-style changed completely after she married Uncle Franz and moved from a large city to a farm area. She had always been a hard worker, but after she moved to Lippborg she worked from dawn to dusk. She took care of her garden from early spring to late autumn. She was proud of her success raising the best vegetables, she enjoyed her abundant harvest and then preserved everything she had raised. Countless labelled jars were lining her pantry shelves. She made marmalades and jams and fruit syrups. She prepared tubs filled with sauerkraut and beans, pickles and pickled vegetables. The late summer was a busy time at Aunt Minchen's house – it resembled a food factory.

My aunt's only means of transportation was her bicycle with a carrier. She and I would bicycle to some of the nearby farms to pick up eggs and butter and whatever the farmers were willing to give her. I loved those early morning bicycle rides on the narrow dirt roads snaking through the tall wheat fields. Uncle Franz owned a motorbike which he used for his business. He and Aunt Minchen would often go by motorbike to the nearest town called Beckum. She put up a courageous front, but she really was scared to death of the thing.

Uncle Franz Nottelmann was born in Lippborg in 1892. He was a tall man, with rather shifty eyes. He had short-cropped, grey-brown hair and usually wore a German-style hunting hat with a feather stuck in the brim. When he worked in his cabinet shop (he was a furniture-maker) he wore overalls, but he was always well dressed when he saw customers. His speech bore strong hints of the Westphalian dialect. In the evening and at weekends he was almost always accompanied by a disreputable friend and drinking companion, also born in Lippborg. Uncle Franz expected and received acknowledgement from my aunt that he was in charge and that his wishes had to be fulfilled without question. In short he was very much the boss. (Uncle Franz's first wife divorced him and they did not have children.)

It had always been a mystery to the family how Aunt Minchen had met Uncle Franz. My aunt was well into her forties when she got married. (My Aunt Mille was convinced that they had met through a newspaper advertisement!)

Uncle Franz was born into a devoutly Catholic family. None of his three sisters lived in Lippborg any more: his mother lived with him and Aunt Minchen in a rented stone house in the centre of the village. The kitchen and pantry and old Mrs Nottelmann's room (Uncle Franz's mother) were on the first floor, as was their dining-cum-living room, 'the good room', used only for special occasions. Their bedroom was on the second floor. The downstairs floors were covered with large tiles, which made the floors quite cold in the winter. Each room except for the bedrooms had a coke- or coal-fired stove. The toilet was outside in a small outhouse. They washed themselves with cold running water at the sink in one of the large pantries.

On bath-day, usually a Saturday, enormous pots of water were heated on the kitchen stove. A metal bathtub was installed in the middle of the kitchen for that occasion, and everybody took their turn as directed by my aunt. I loved these baths. Aunt Minchen would fuss over me and brush my back with a large soft brush, and when I was finished she would wrap me in a huge towel. The kitchen was wonderfully warm since the stove was fired up to capacity. Aunt Minchen would take advantage of the heated ovens and she would usually bake bread and cakes on Saturdays. A delightful aroma permeated the house – I can smell it still.

Aunt Minchen had substantial savings when she married Uncle Franz. He needed her money to get out of debt as he had overextended himself by buying several pieces of very expensive machinery and other equipment. He also wanted to buy the house they were living in, which he did, thereby mortgaging himself beyond his capacity to stay afloat financially. His worst problems were his drinking and womanizing. He frequented several taverns with some of his women friends, who were notorious in the village.

And yet, with all these terrible shortcomings, he never objected to any help my aunt gave us, even though he was fully aware of our background. Indeed, later on he gave safe haven to my mother when she needed it. His own mother 'old Mrs Nottelmann', as she was usually referred to, hated the Nazis, and she became a very good friend and protector of my mother. Unfortunately, the relationship between her and Aunt Minchen was not always so good. Aunt Minchen felt that she and some of Uncle Franz's relatives, especially his sisters, resented her because she was not a Catholic. I think that she might subconsciously have blamed Mrs Nottelmann for her son's transgressions. I know that during the worst

Nazi years Uncle Franz, completely decked out in his Nazi regalia, told my mother, 'Lina, I won't let you down!', and he kept that promise. So whenever I think of Uncle Franz I have very mixed feelings.

6 · *How Can We Get Out?*

By 1936 even the most optimistic among the Jews could no longer fool themselves. I often overheard my parents talking about people who had been arrested and were never heard from again. There was fear and foreboding in their subdued voices, but I did not think that it could get much worse. I also had enormous confidence in their judgement, and I was sure that they would find a way out of this.

Properties, businesses, financial holdings and Jewish cultural institutions were now all being confiscated by the Nazis. Almost daily new directives and proclamations were being issued against us. It was at this point that my parents decided to emigrate. They considered many countries and regions of the world: the climate, the language and in particular how one could fit in and make a living there to support a family with two children. They would get so enthusiastic about a certain country – they would read all about it, consult the atlas and even began to study the language – only to learn that they would not qualify as immigrants. Some countries would issue visas to farmers and mechanics but not to businessmen; other countries required more assets than my parents could muster. Some countries gave visas only to young, single people, and so it went on: their hopes would rise only to be dashed over and over again. They worried that they would not be able to acclimatize to some tropical regions, and so, night after night, we travelled all over the globe.

After making enquiries on how to enter the United States, my parents wrote to a distant relative in Chicago, a Mr Morris Beifus, and asked him to supply an affidavit for us. Anybody who wanted to immigrate into the United States had to obtain a pledge from a relative who was a US citizen, stating that they, the sponsor, would assume the total financial responsibility for the new immigrant until he became financially self-sufficient so that he would not become a burden to the state. This declaration, which had to be backed by adequate financial resources, was the all important affidavit. An applicant would receive a number on the waiting list of prospective immigrants from the consulate. In 1936/37 it took a year or two after the issuance of a number before one was given an interview with the consul to request a visa for immigration into the United States.

The Beifuses were wealthy people, and even though they were flooded by requests from other relatives, they did give us an affidavit. My parents received a number from the consulate and they waited a very long time before they were called to appear before the consul. He then determined that the Beifus family had given so many affidavits that my parents needed to procure additional pledges. This meant starting the whole procedure all over again.

By now it was 1938. They approached another relative in San Antonio, Texas, for a supplemental affidavit, but without success. This man from San Antonio used to visit us in Germany before the Nazis came to power. He was an alcoholic and he never forgave anybody who did not drink with him. My father was sure that he had wrecked his chances with him years before.

In 1936, after our arrival in Düsseldorf, both my brother and I attended the private Jewish school there. This school had an outstanding reputation, and I found it much more demanding than my school in Dortmund had been. I was completely uninterested in my Hebrew studies, and I think, at least partly so, because my father made no secret of his indifference. He showed great interest in my other subjects, especially English and Spanish. I liked this school a great deal and I made many friends there. I did well, especially in those subjects that engaged my attention.

My father's cousin Karl Kohn was fluent in many languages, and he tutored me in both English and Spanish several times a week. The Kohns owned a big hardware store across from my grandmother's house on Friedrichstrasse. They had a beautifully furnished, large apartment on the top floor of the building. Uncle 'Jupp' Kohn, Uncle Karl's father, was my Grandmother Lenneberg's cousin. He was a widower. Three of his sons, Alfred, Paul and Karl were running the business. Another son, Siegfried, was married to his non-Jewish wife Hilde. Fräulein Frankenberg was the Kohn's housekeeper, and had been with them so very long that she was part of the family. This then was the place where I learned English and enjoyed Fräulein Frankenberg's cookies.

I admired Uncle Karl very much. He was an excellent teacher. I was always eagerly looking forward to my lessons with him. It was a challenge and a fun way to learn a language. Our expected immigration to America gave me a lot of incentive.

The 'Kohn-boys', as they were usually referred to, were unmarried, all three had had long relationships with non-Jewish women. Uncle Karl had been supporting a Viennese lady friend for many years. She lived in a luxurious apartment near the bank of the River Rhine. Their father had made it clear that he would never give his consent for them to marry their non-Jewish women; they also knew that if they disobeyed his wishes he would most likely disinherit them. Nor was Siegfried's marriage to his wife Hilde many years earlier welcomed by his father, who never recognized his daughter-in-law nor did he take his son Siegfried into his business.

The edicts of Nuremberg in 1935 not only forbade Jews to marry gentiles but also made it very dangerous for them to continue their relationships. This, of course, affected the Kohns. Paul and his future wife fled to Holland, where he converted to Catholicism. They married and both survived in Maastricht. Uncle Karl's friend moved back to Vienna after she was repeatedly visited by the Gestapo; it became too dangerous for them to continue living together.*

My parents became good friends with Siegfried and Hilde Kohn,‡ and in 1938 they seriously considered emigrating with

---

* Uncle Karl Kohn, his brother Alfred, their father Jupp and Fräulein Frankenberg all perished in the camps.

‡ Siegfried Kohn and his Christian wife Hilde survived the Nazi persecution in Germany.

them to South America – Uruguay or Paraguay – to work there in agriculture. It seemed to be their last hope of leaving Germany. My parents and the Kohns would meet almost every evening to finalize their plans. Maps were spread on the floor, they read, discussed and argued. Unfortunately, they were taken in by some dishonest scheme. (I remember the young man well, who identified himself as a South American agent who could facilitate their immigration plans.) This scheme followed the pattern of all the others: high hopes at the outset, study of the country into which we were going to immigrate, plans to study the language, and then finally every effort failed and our hopes were destroyed. We were stuck in Germany. It was too late!

I had made friends and I became politically aware at a very young age because the politics and the racial persecution in Nazi Germany affected us every day. I joined a Jewish youth group and became a Zionist. Our members visited Jewish families and urged them to contribute money to help plant trees in Palestine.

I fasted on Yom Kippur, and I was outraged when some of my friends pretended to be fasting for the benefit of their parents but broke their fast as soon as their parents had turned their backs. I am sure that my parents were upset about my religious fervour.

I also became a voracious reader. My new addiction was a writer by the name of Karl May, who wrote innumerable novels about the adventures of cowboys and Indians of the American West. He was a great writer and described America in fascinating language, even though he had never left Germany. Many readers like me were addicted to his books.

In 1937 school was very rigorous. We still had excellent teachers, but gradually we lost many who were able to immigrate into other countries. Their replacements were less exciting and some like Mr Emanuel were unable to maintain discipline. He lost us the minute he stepped into the classroom with his pronouncement 'Order, discipline and manners must prevail in any classroom!' (*Ordnung, Zucht und Sitte muss in jeder Mitte einer Klasse sein*). Somebody called him 'Tante Emma', I don't know why, and that name stayed with him. Our school meant a lot to us, it was our anchor and place where we felt secure, and a place where we could still have fun.

The mood in the Jewish community was mostly one of shock and disbelief as diktats with new restrictions and orders were constantly being announced by the Nazi authorities. The table-talk and conversations with friends centred solely on 'How can we get out?'. Every day the situation grew more desperate for German Jews, but it also became obvious that Germany was preparing for war. As time went on into the late 1930s, many had exhausted all avenues to leave Germany, and we were among them, but we were still hoping against hope that we would find a country that would take us. My father worked day and night to find an open door: he travelled to Holland and Belgium but all to no avail. (He usually returned with Dutch butter and Belgian chocolates!)

In 1933 my parents and many of their Jewish friends had been convinced that Hitler would not be in power for very long, they argued that the German people would not allow it! I think that up until November 1938 they were hoping for a miracle to occur. Then came the so-called 'Kristallnacht' when countless Germans watched and many applauded as Jewish homes were openly plundered and destroyed. Jewish shopfronts were smashed and our school and synagogue were burned to the ground. Jewish men were beaten and arrested (my father was in hiding, while some of his friends were badly beaten). It became quite clear what the Nazis were capable of, and now everybody was desperate to leave Germany.

Since our school no longer existed, my father enrolled my nine-year-old brother in a private Jewish school in Duisburg, one of the few Jewish places of learning which was still functioning. It was a long journey by train for the boy. Two of our teachers, Herr Kurt Schnook and his wife, were still in Düsseldorf, and they organized classes for the older students on the premises of a large laundry facility which was located on the outskirts of Düsseldorf. These laundry buildings, which were owned by the Ellsberg family, became our school for many months. The grounds surrounding the laundry became our soccer field, our gymnasium and playground. We took part in all kinds of sports activities and competitions. Our parents and the Schnooks made a heroic effort to give us some semblance of education and normal life.

It was frightening when we saw with our own eyes, and often heard on the radio, the huge assembled crowds shouting *'Heil Hitler!'* with enthusiasm, their arms raised high in the Hitler salute. Young and old alike, ready to own the whole world, and we had no place in that world.

Signs saying 'JEWS NOT WELCOME' (*Juden unerwünscht*) could now be seen everywhere: in shop windows, cinemas, cafés, theatres, restaurants, beauty parlours and all kinds of public facilities such as libraries, museums and swimming pools. My brother and I were intrigued by the famous American Mouse, but alas we could only glance at the colourful posters of Mickey playing the piano which were on display in the large glass boxes outside the cinema.

Jews were dismissed from state schools, high schools and universities. A new decree instructed all Jews to appear at their local police station to receive new identifications, namely yellow pieces of cloth with a black Star of David and the word Jew (*Jude*) in Hebraicized letters printed on it. These Jewish stars (*Judensterne*) or Stars of David had to be sewn on every outer garment and they had to be prominently displayed whenever a Jew was entering the German world outside his home. In addition, every male Jew, regardless of age, had to sign his name with the middle name Israel and every female had to use the name Sara as a middle name. All identification papers were changed with the addition of these middle names. We were now an openly marked people.

I wore the yellow star with dignity but I felt uncomfortable entering any store or building because I never knew if a merchant would refuse to sell to me, or if someone would use abusive language while passing me in the street – or worse, beat me up. In the winter I tried to leave the house before dusk before the evening curfew came into effect. I walked very close to buildings and tried to protect myself from the hostile stares of passers-by that would invariably follow me. One afternoon I was confronted by a uniformed group of

Hitler Youth who heckled me with the following verses (this is a free translation):

Jew Isaac	*Jude Itzig*
Pointy shnozz	*Nase spitzig*
Angular eyes	*Augen eckig*
Filthy ass.	*Arschloch dreckig.*

Travel became almost impossible for us and was soon completely prohibited. Anybody who was caught not following these orders would be subject to severe beatings by the Gestapo. The usual procedure, however, was immediate arrest and imprisonment. As yet, concentration camps had not become part of our vocabulary.

7 · The War Begins

In 1938 Hitler annexed Austria (the Anschluss) and as a result of the Munich agreement, the Sudetenland was ceded to him. In March 1939 he marched into Moravia and Bohemia. It became clearer each day that war was inevitable.

Our last apartment in Düsseldorf was located in a building which was owned by a Jewish family. It was directly opposite and on the same level as the railway tracks, so we could watch the trains from our window at Halskestrasse 12. (I can still see and hear the long trains rolling by with military recruits singing the old and the new songs of soldiers going to war, leaving their sweethearts and marching far into the unknown, fighting for their fatherland and for glory.) Day and night freight trains carrying tanks and military equipment carefully covered with huge tarpaulins went rumbling by. This was 1939 and the trains were going east and the news told us in September of that year that Germany had invaded Poland. The war had started.

At about this time my father received orders to work as a labourer in heavy construction from early morning to late at night. My mother continued to work in the leather factory, I kept house and my brother still commuted to Duisburg to get some schooling. The Ellsberg's laundry buildings had been taken over by the Nazis and our limited schooling had to cease altogether. I received private tutoring from Herr Schnook – he and his wife were probably the only teachers left in Düsseldorf who had taught at our school before it was burned down. I continued my language instruction with Uncle Karl. Food was being rationed now and our ration cards had 'Jew' (*Jude*) stamped across every coupon.

By 1940 most of my friends had left. I became acquainted with a group of young people who were several years older than me. I was only 14, but I already carried a lot of responsibility and, because of the difficult time in which I had grown up, I had matured far beyond my age. I met a young man whom my Uncle Karl Kohn fully approved of, and so Kurt Eckstein and I became very good friends. He was eighteen, good-looking, and I especially liked his dark, warm eyes and his sense of humour. He was an only child and lived with his father: his mother was dead. He was an intelligent, highly principled, considerate young man. He also took English lessons with my Uncle Karl. He had been training to become a car mechanic, hoping that a trade would afford him a better chance for emigration.

Kurt's best friends were two brothers, both of whom were tall, blond, handsome and bright. They were living with their Jewish mother and grandmother; their non-Jewish father had died. They owned a Victrola (gramophone) and Kurt tried to teach me how to dance. We had few social outlets, our get-togethers at our apartments were our only diversion. I enjoyed getting dressed up for our small parties. I was very proud of my beautiful blue hat which my mother had managed to acquire for me. I liked nice clothes like any girl of my age, but the yellow star, prominently displayed on my outer clothing, took all the incentive out of shopping, strolling in the parks or going anywhere that brought me in contact with people. Consumer goods were becoming scarcer and most items were being rationed now. After a shop assistant had refused to serve me, I avoided entering shops as much as possible.

I was almost fifteen, but I was quite naïve about sex. I remember very well a party at Ruth's house (the girlfriend of the elder of the two brothers). It was New Year's Eve. I watched his hands as they were sliding under Ruth's skirt, exploring and caressing her. I just did not know how to react. I was not shocked, I just thought it odd that she let him do that. I judged her quite harshly, and I was convinced that she was 'one of those girls'. My friend Kurt tried to shield me from the ongoing performance, and told me not to pay any attention to them. (He was very protective of me.) When I related the incident to my mother, she convinced me that Ruth had a questionable reputation and she called her a 'loose woman'. I am glad that Ruth enjoyed the short time she had with her man, as not too many months later she was deported to Minsk. This was the beginning of 1942.

When Kurt and his two friends, their mother and Ruth received notices from the Gestapo that they had to assemble at the *Schlachthof* (slaughterhouse) in Düsseldorf for deportation to a labour camp, it signalled the beginning of the end for all of us. I was shattered to lose Kurt, but I also felt an awful premonition that terrible things were going to happen. We were trapped. Rumours circulated in what was left of the Jewish community that unspeakable conditions existed in these so-called labour camps. My parents were depressed; they made heroic efforts to shield us, but occasionally we caught the words 'Polish camps' from their conversation – though they did not believe these 'rumours'.

We were social outcasts shunned by our fellow German citizens, some through conviction, others because of fear. The result was the same for us. The yellow star on our clothing identified us instantly and made us constantly vulnerable to physical and verbal attack. The food coupons with 'Jew' (*Jude*) stamped on them, now gave the grocers the option not to sell to us at all. We had to use our new middle name whenever we gave our name or signed anything. Anybody who did not fully comply with these rules was subjected to beatings or worse – arrest.

It was a terrible shock when our bicycles were confiscated in early 1942. I loved my bicycle, and it was a very important means of transport for me as I used it to do our family's grocery shopping. (I preferred to avoid public transport.) Not a week passed without new demands and restrictions.

Kurt and his friends were gone, and I never heard from them again. Kurt's friends' grandmother was all alone now and I kept my promise and visited her very often. This old lady was grieving for her daughter and grandsons. It was pitiful.

Food was getting scarcer now, everything was rationed. My Aunt Minchen was married now and lived in a small village not too far from the Dutch border. Lippborg was located in the centre of a large German farm area. She sent us enormous baskets of potatoes, cabbage, beets, carrots, fruits and whatever else she could find. My mother and I invented new recipes, substituting potatoes and farina for wheatflour which was unavailable. A friend of my mother's sold meat to her which she had obtained on the black market.

My Uncle Erich (my father's oldest brother, who was married to his Catholic wife Erna) had been working at the Jewish Community Centre since he and his mother lost their store to the Nazis. He had access to all the records there and he removed his son Paul's name from the Jewish birth register. He and his wife Erna were successful in having Paul's name entered in the Catholic birth records. He himself had also converted to the Catholic religion unbeknown to us. My father approached him in 1941 to remove my brother's and my name as well but he insisted that he could not do that. (He was probably correct: he might have jeopardized himself and his family if he had done so.) This religious switch gave his son Paul 'preferential mixed-race status' designation (*Priviligierter Mischling*), which shielded him and his brother and sisters, who were born during the worst Nazi years, from many restrictions and ultimately from deportation.

Our widowed friend Frau Wallach had returned from visiting her sons in Palestine before the war broke out. She felt that she was too old to adjust to life on the Kibbutz. She darned our socks and helped with the ironing and she often took her meals with us. The Gestapo put Frau Wallach into one of the first transports leaving Düsseldorf. She did not survive.

8 · *Halskestrasse*

The apartment building in which we lived at the corner of Halskestrasse in Düsseldorf had a grocery store at street level. It was five storeys high: there was one apartment each on the second, third and fourth floors and two apartments on the top floor under the roof. There was a large laundry room in the cellar where every tenant kept his or her own manual wringer-type washing machine; we boiled our wash in a large wash-kettle which was heated by a coal fire. The wash had to be carried up many flights of stairs to the attic drying room. Every tenant had a small storage area in the basement where we stored our coal, potatoes and preserved food.

Our apartment was on the third floor. All five rooms were located off a long corridor reminiscent of a railway carriage. The large kitchen was the centre of our family life. We still had some of our furniture and a few precious paintings and rugs. Every window faced the tracks of the large rail network leading to and from the main junction of the city's railway stations. Because our apartment was located at the same height as the tracks, the trains were with us all the time, their black soot bellowing from their smoke stacks accompanied by the ever present clanking of the wheels interrupted only occasionally by the sound of blowing steam whistles.

I remember a few families very well. The Wiegands lived on the second floor, the von Staars lived above us. The Rosenbuschs and Müllers lived under the roof. The Müllers were very primitive, dirty poor people. Herr Müller worked as a labourer; they had five children and Frau Müller was pregnant every nine months: she was a sorry sight, a real Käthe Kollwitz figure. My father would often carry her coal pails up from the basement into her attic apartment. She always looked unkempt, undernourished, with blonde,

44

straggly hair, bad teeth and a large stomach. She did not mind it when we fed her children, and she did not show any open hostility to us. Her husband was a short, squat, swarthy, unfriendly man, who never greeted us and always looked the other way when we met on the stairs.

The Rosenbuschs occupied the second of the attic apartments. They had no children. She was a tall good-looking woman with a strong Bavarian accent. They both worked. Herr Rosenbusch was an electrician. He was an intelligent, ruggedly handsome self-made man and a convinced communist. The Rosenbuschs despised the Nazis, and Mr Rosenbusch would listen to the British broadcasts on his short-wave radio. This, of course, was very dangerous, and if caught he would have been sent to a concentration camp or worse. Once the air raids started, the Rosenbuschs, who never went into the shelter, used that opportunity to listen to the English broadcasts. Very often, particularly during the worst raids, they would ask my father to join them. My father always insisted that my mother, my brother and I seek the safety of the air raid shelter in the basement of our building. He never did so himself.

We felt extremely uncomfortable in the shelter. We always stayed near the door as we could not mingle with our Aryan neighbours. We felt like outcasts. Frau Wiegand, a good-looking woman of about 30 with two children, seemed to be sympathetic to us. Her husband, a German soldier who was stationed in occupied France, sent enormously large boxes of wine and other stolen goods home. I remember that Mrs Wiegand once spoke out against the Nazis and the war during a particularly severe air attack. We were too scared to look at her or anybody else in the shelter. Huddling in a corner with as much distance as possible between and us and our fellow tenants, we pretended not to listen and not to hear. The middle-aged couple on the third floor eventually avoided all contact with us.

My parents became very ill and it was discovered that I was a diphtheria carrier. I had infected them even though I did not become ill myself, but my father almost died. My parents were bedridden with high fever, and my Grandmother Lenneberg brought us food, especially chicken soup and noodle *kugel* – one of her specialties. She left the containers in front of our apartment door to avoid contracting the infection herself.

My mother was now the sole breadwinner of the family. My father was paid either very little or nothing. (I cannot recall if he was paid at all for his forced labour construction work.) Our family started to feel the pinch financially and my parents sold a number of paintings, rugs and valuable porcelain to former employees for very little money. Bit by bit we lost all our possessions.

In 1941 and 1942 the State Secret Police (Gestapo or Geheime Staatspolizei) confiscated almost everything of value. They would make frequent unannounced visits to Jewish homes and searched, seized and destroyed whatever they could lay their hands on. They looked for 'forbidden' books and they punished their owners if any such books were found. I can still see my father in the wash cellar burning his prized books, his friends as he called them, in the oven under the big laundry kettle for fear that they might be found in a Gestapo raid. These were books by famous writers and poets who for one reason or another were on the 'forbidden' book list. Possession of books by all Jewish and many non-Jewish authors was enough to put one into prison. The proscribed list read like 'Who's Who' in poetry and literature.

My mother received an order to present herself at the Gestapo offices. After some questioning, Gestapo officer Pütz told her to divorce the Jew, or else! My mother simply refused. Herr Pütz curtly dismissed her, and my mother was keenly aware of his hatred and anger. He continued his surveillance of her even after my father and brother and I had been deported.

1. Oma Schneider, 54, in 1922.

2. Lina Schneider and Otto
   Lenneberg, 1924.

3. Oma Lenneberg and Ursula, 1931.

4. Opa Schneider and Ursula, 1931.

5. My first day at School, 1932.

6. Otto Lenneberg, ca. 1937.

7. Ursula's brother, Walter Lenneberg, 1939.

8. Buschi, Holland 1946.

9. Ursula, X-ray technician, 1948.

10. Hans and Ursula Pawel, 1948.

11. Oma Schneider and Tante Mille, 1950.

12. Caroline Lenneberg-Bruenell, neé Schneider, ca. 1950.

13. Caroline (Lina) and Siegmund Bruenell, ca. 1959.

14. Tante Minchen and Onkel Franz Nottelmann, ca. 1960.

15. David and Bruce Pawel, 1963.

16. Reunion in Los Angeles, 1975. From left to right: Ursula, Buschi, Hannah and Zdena.

17. Hans and Ursula Pawel, 1997.

18. Theresienstadt 'fake' money, distributed during 'Beautification' for the Red Cross in the spring of 1944.

9 · *Deportation*

During the middle of July 1942 I received a notice from the Gestapo headquarters in Düsseldorf ordering me to present myself on Monday, 20 July 1942 at the Düsseldorf slaughterhouse (*Schlachthof*) to join a transport to a labour camp. My father and mother were very upset but I did not fully understand the impact of this order. My parents had long discussions: should they let me go alone, or should they and my brother volunteer to go with me so that we could keep our family together. They were convinced that my father and my brother would be ordered into some future transportation, quite possibly to other camps. Then our family would be separated and scattered, each one of us left to fend for himself. They finally decided to volunteer to accompany me. The Gestapo denied my mother's request, but allowed the other three of us to leave together.

Each of us took a suitcase which had been packed and unpacked many times (these suitcases had originally been purchased to accompany us to the United States). An old tailor friend of my mother's made warm coats for us from very heavy, woollen material, which she had obtained on the black market by bartering some of her jewellery. She worried terribly that it might be very cold in the east, particularly during winter, where we most likely would end up in a labour camp. My mother spent day and night before our departure adding this and that to our luggage. She tried to put on a brave face, but she was devastated. The Nazis tore her heart out by separating us from her. My parents must have been through a terrible conflict as to whether their decision was the right one. How does one assess this? It was like a lottery. It was the wrong decision for my father and my brother, but who knows, there probably was no right decision for my parents to make.

My parents had impressed on my brother and on me that if we became separated we should return to my Aunt Minchen's house in Lippborg, where we would all be reunited after the war had ended – 'After the criminal is out!' (*Wenn der Verbrecher ab ist!*) A sentence which had been repeated over and over again, like a daily prayer.

So it was that on Monday, 20 July 1942, we arrived at the Düsseldorf slaughterhouse. Our luggage was taken from us to be shipped in the baggage cars. We were ordered to register at stations manned by Gestapo and SS and we were given identifying tags to wear around our neck. We took our hand-luggage into the train compartment. Bella, a nurse in her twenties, and her friend, a physician who had been a radiologist in Düsseldorf, were also on the train. They befriended me and included me in their conversation: most of their interests were medically orientated and their 'shop talk' fascinated me. I think they planted the first thought that I might someday want to work in the medical field.

Two days later, on 22 July, we reached Bauschowitz (Bohusovice), the station where all transports to Theresienstadt (Terezin) arrived. It was a very hot day and we had to walk under the burning sun from Bauschowitz to Theresienstadt. Theresienstadt is located in Bohemia, roughly midway between Dresden and Prague. I have no clear memory of how long that walk took – it may have been one and a half hours. We were only allowed to carry our hand-luggage. We were constantly being shouted at by the SS: '*Schneller machen!*' (Get going! Faster! Move on!)

Jewish workers unloaded the freight cars, all our luggage was loaded onto hand-carts and trucks. The whole workforce was comprised of Jewish forced labour, mostly Czech – all inmates of the ghetto. We never saw our luggage or rucksacks again.

Many sick and elderly people were in our transport and they found it impossible to keep up with the pace set by the SS on this very long, arduous walk with no shade and no water. They were sweltering in the sun on this hot July day. Some of them were hoisted into open trucks and delivered into the ghetto like cattle. Our feelings were numbed when we entered Theresienstadt. The shouting of the SS, the efficient way in which we were herded along, the eager cooperation of the Jewish workers emptying the train and unloading our luggage – all this gave us a feeling of unreality. We could not yet comprehend that we were here – and what it all meant.

We, the arrivals of this transport, were all herded into a holding barracks called Aussiger Kaserne, commonly referred to as the sluice (*die Schleuse*). (The SS designated the area where people arriving into or being transported out of the ghetto were being held as *die Schleuse*.) A thousand people were herded into these damp, whitewashed underground vaults of the large barracks. Tall SS men dressed in their smart uniforms and shining boots, many with whips in their hands, supervised the inmates who had to do their dirty work. They made sure that the operation functioned efficiently. They inspected our hand-luggage and made body searches. If money or anything of value was found, it was immediately confiscated. Many people were overcome by the heat and fainted. Whatever we had left in our hand-luggage had to be guarded since some of our own people were not averse to stealing from the new arrivals. One could hardly blame them, everything was valuable – even a sewing needle and thread. People were deprived of the most basic necessities. After all moneys and jewellery had been taken from us, we were assigned to our new quarters. Men and women were separated. My father and my brother were assigned to Q613.

The streets in the camp were laid out in a rectangular pattern. The L-streets (for *Längsstrassen*) ran in one (lengthwise) direction with the Q-Streets (for *Querstrassen*, that is, cross-streets) crossing them at right angles.

Early the following morning I started to search for Q613 to find my father and brother. Walking through the streets of the ghetto, I saw a town with many barracks, stables and old stone or stucco-and-timber houses. Everybody I passed was a fellow prisoner. They all wore the yellow Star of David and the word *Jude* in black Hebracized letters printed inside the star. I could not understand their language as they all spoke Czech. When I asked directions in German, they answered in

Czech that they could not understand me. A large, open limousine with SS men drove through the street passing me. I finally reached Q613 where I found my father and my brother in a small, empty room (about three by five metres), devoid of beds or furniture. They shared this cubicle with eight other men, and had all to sleep on the floor. Only much later did they receive three-storey bunk-beds.

I was assigned to quarters even smaller than those of my father and brother in the barrack of L415. The barrack was an old multi-level stone structure with long corridors, labyrinths and archways and vaulted ceilings. The thick, damp, peeling walls had once been whitewashed. The room I shared with eight other women was more like a passageway between the hall and an adjacent room. It had no windows or ventilation and was located next to a smelly toilet. We would allude to this often unbearable stench as 'zeroche, die Höhenluft' (zeroche = bad smell in Yiddish; Höhenluft = pure mountain air in German), and our sarcastic humour (Galgenhumor) helped us to cope. My only possessions consisted of a small hiking bag and the clothing I wore.

Curfew! (Strassensperre), and everybody had to remain indoors. This was a frequent occurrence, enforced whenever a transport arrived or left the ghetto, but it often meant that a large contingent of SS were descending on every building, house and barrack to check every room, every bunk, and to make body searches of people suspected of hiding valuables or money. Occasionally we heard rumours that somebody had tried to escape, then the SS would punish the whole ghetto with Strassensperre and house-to-house searches. We were frightened: it showed in our faces, in our eyes, and the Germans liked to torment us to amuse themselves – it was their game, we were their pawns.

Other prisoners cautioned us early on: 'Don't trust strangers – even fellow prisoners may actually be spies planted in the ghetto by the SS.'

Food was very poor and insufficient and got progressively worse. During the first year almost all of our bread rations were mouldy. The half-rotten and mostly unwashed potatoes were cooked in their skins in large vats.

The ghetto could not cope with the swelling population. Theresienstadt originally had less than 10,000 inhabitants but in the summer of 1942 it had to absorb 60,000 people. The result was outbreaks of scarlet fever, infectious hepatitis, diarrhoea, typhoid and paratyphoid, TB, encephalitis, scabies, impetigo and more – and all this accompanied by bed bugs and lice. Every day 150 to 200 people died.

My father worked at the building shed, constructing coffins. Later he was promoted to being a fully fledged carpenter. I too worked at the building shed for one week and then found work as an assistant at the Children's Welfare Service. I had to take the kindergarten children to the *Bastei* – the earthen wall which encircled and originally protected this military settlement town. I had to look after all the children's needs from dawn to dusk and often during the night. The children called me 'Uschi', a common short form of my name; it is still what many of my friends call me today.

I still vividly remember this small garrison town, located in a valley surrounded by beautiful, majestic mountains. I enjoyed my walks high up on the embankment. From there I could see all the magnificent mountains and watch the white clouds skimming their tops. From that high place I would gain strength, and dream and hope that some day I should be free again. There, up on the *Bastei*, stood an old oak. I loved that tree – it inspired me. I was awed by it and would gaze quietly at it. It was my talisman. I sometimes wonder if it is still there.

10 · Theresienstadt (1)

My brother was sent to the Youth Home in a barrack which was called the *Scola* (school). His *Betreuer* (person charged with educational and general care of the children in his or her room, practically a surrogate parent) was Louis Lowy, a compassionate, intelligent, able young teacher. My brother loved Louis. Louis Lowy, Hilde Dublon, Kurt Kohorn, Kurt Rosenbaum, Sigi Kwasniewski and others, most of them in their very early twenties, were instrumental in starting the Home for Youth (*Jugendheim*) in the barrack L414 in September 1942. In this new arrangement I was assigned to assist Hilde Dublon in our room, Home 5 (*Heim* 5).

Hilde was a tall, beautiful, highly intelligent young woman from Hamburg. She had been transported to Theresienstadt with her mother, who was living in another part of the ghetto. Mother and daughter were devoted to each other. Hilde and I lived with and took care of 30 teenage girls in a barrack room, in which three-storey bunk-beds lined the walls and a large table with benches occupied the centre. We were given some clothing with little regard to proper size.

The luggage from every transport was confiscated and the contents were sorted by prisoners. All the good clothing and anything of value was sent to Germany; what remained was distributed to the inmates. Everybody received a dish, a metal cup, a spoon and a fork. The food was dispensed from a big vat into our food containers outside the kitchen. The food was uniform for all prisoners in this Jewish town. The soups were a watery mixture, and the potatoes were cooked in their dirty skins. Sometimes our meal consisted of a flour dumpling called *Knedliky* with a sugary sauce. A strange black juice made from chicory was called coffee. We individually received our black bread rations and 'marmalade' (some artificially concocted spread).

My father worked in the carpentry shop. He was very skilful and well liked, and since he was able to do favours for others by building useful items for them, he was often the recipient of extra food which he shared with us. He managed to obtain large containers of food like puddings and thick soups – foods which were beyond the imagination of most ghetto-dwellers. I am sure that he worked very hard to please the cooks and kitchen personnel. Working as a skilled labourer and always in the open air kept my father vigorous and in excellent health. I do not remember that he suffered from a single cold in the two years he spent in Theresienstadt and other work assignments.

The Czech Jews had come to Theresienstadt before any of the other prisoners, consequently most of the desirable jobs were held by them. Inmates with the right connections enjoyed privileged treatment. We had no connections: we were just lucky to end up in much better housing and work than most. The Czech Jews all spoke German but many refused to admit that they even understood it. They hated everything German and that included us, the German Jews. Our language problem was a terrible barrier, especially when we first arrived in the ghetto.

Since our Youth Home was located in the barrack L414, it was always referred to as L414. It was densely populated but we had access to showers. We were among young people who withstood the harsh conditions much better than the elderly. We concentrated on getting some education in spite of it all, and we were much more optimistic that we would eventually be freed and that we would survive.

Some of the barrack rooms of L414 were inhabited by young adults of about sixteen to twenty-five who worked elsewhere during the day, some in factories and others in the nearby fields.

Transports from all over Germany, Holland and all the annexed lands were arriving almost daily. My grandmother Lenneberg arrived not too long after we did. I visited her daily in her horrible living quarters, in the attic space of an old house. However, she was assigned a very small sleeping area on a rough, old wooden attic floor, barely large enough to spread her blanket. She seemed completely resigned to die.

She contracted diarrhoea shortly after her arrival. She never asked how we were managing. Her one great fear was that her grandson Paul (Paulchen), my cousin, would also be sent to Theresienstadt.

There was a remarkable amount of talent at L414. Louis Lowy was a great teacher, a very knowledgeable young man who was totally dedicated to his charges. Many of the *Betreuer* were bright people who contributed to the various seminars which we eagerly attended. The incentive to learn was very strong, all the more because the SS did their utmost to prevent any education from taking place.

Sigi Kwasniewski, a young intellectual who came from Czechoslovakia, was the head of the Youth Home. His secretary, Herr Jakob, was a deeply Orthodox Jew; Pani Klinkeova, a Czech opera singer, also worked in the office (the *Kanzlei*). She sang in the ghetto production of the popular opera *The Bartered Bride* by Smetana. (She usually practised her arias in the toilet.) Pani Klinke's mother was a short lady with silver-grey hair which she had braided and twisted into a huge bun. The old lady possessed an enormous, glorious voice. I shall always remember her rendition of 'Ave Maria'. Her stage was any place: the corridors of the barrack, the courtyard, the attic and, of course, the toilet!

Helly Halberstadt somehow managed to keep her accordion. She had a sizeable repertoire of songs from around the world. She was able to transcribe many classical music pieces and play them on her accordion. I particularly remember how beautifully she played Brahms' 'Hungarian Dances'. We sang many Hebrew songs and she would accompany us. She was marvellous: I admired her so much.

Whenever we attended seminars, gathered for free discussions, or were entertained, several people stood guard so that they could send warning signals in case the SS decided to raid or search the barracks late at night. All these activities, especially large gatherings, were strictly prohibited (*verboten*). Everybody was afraid to be caught by the SS doing something that was '*verboten*'.

Any inmate who attempted to send mail to the outside – except for the censored postcards everybody was encouraged to send at specifically prescribed times – anybody who kept money, valuables, jewellery or cigarettes, and was caught, was severely punished. This would most likely mean time in the 'Little Fortress' (*die kleine Festung*). The very mention of the name put fear into all of us. Prisoners were tortured and killed there. They were kept in solitary confinement, and if they were not hanged or shot right there, they would be soon transported to other camps, the most likely being Auschwitz.

I had a very good rapport with Hilde Dublon, the senior *Betreuer* of our room and we worked well together. Hilde was in her early twenties, well-educated, capable and caring. She and I shared a double bunk on the third tier. We also shared the work taking care of our charges, and even though I was only sixteen, I had been able to handle responsibility for a long time.

In October 1942 I caught scarlet fever from one of the girls, and I spent several weeks in the hospital barrack, which was called '*Spital*'. My neighbour had infectious hepatitis, so I caught that on top of the scarlet fever. Our eyes looked yellow and our urine was brown – that was all that was needed to make a diagnosis. I did not feel very ill, and I received extra rations of sugar and marmalade. I recovered completely thanks to two wonderful Czech physicians who performed miracles with inventive measures since they were given very few supplies and practically no drugs. Whilst I was ill, my grandmother Lenneberg died.

I remember Chanukkah 1942. I was back in my room at L414 and we played *Dreidel*. A *Dreidel* is a top that is spun on a flat surface: it is a game of chance played during the Chanukkah festival. A wonderful first package from my mother arrived, containing, among other things, chocolates, which I shared amongst my 30 girls.

At about this time transports were arriving daily from Vienna, Berlin, Prague, Holland and later on from Denmark. My Aunt Erna, my father's sister, arrived from Frankfurt with her husband, Uncle Fritz. They were, of course, separated and their living conditions were just as bad as my grandmother's had been. I loved Tante Erna and Onkel Fritz very much, and I felt awful that we were living so much more comfortably than they were. I felt so helpless. I visited Tante Erna often. She was suffering from psoriasis and had scratched her arms open – the itching must have been intolerable.

Uncle Fritz was a very tall, well-built man who was used to working with his hands. He did manual labour in the ghetto and seemed to cope well until he came down with pneumonia from which he died. I visited Aunt Erna even more often after Uncle Fritz's death, but I had the feeling that she had lost her will to live. A transport took her to Poland and we never saw her again.

During the winter of 1942/43 a number of young people in our room as well as in other rooms of L414 were running fevers, had bowel problems, complained of aches and pains and developed rashes. Hilde did not feel well either: she had no appetite. She would try her food and I would finish it for her. She was getting weaker every day and had blood in her stools. One day, to our shock, she died, as did a number of the children in the home, including some in our room.

The diagnosis was typhus carried by lice. This was not paratyphus. This was the real killer, a highly contagious disease. I did not get sick, even though I had finished the left-overs from Hilde's plate and had slept in the bunk next to her. We were all scared and devastated. Our first order of business was a huge cleansing campaign. Everybody's clothing was inspected, especially the seams, since lice deposit their eggs in the seams of clothing. The German name for this species of lice is *Kleiderläuse*. Everyone's hair was washed with a vinegar mixture. My girls were inspected every day. Every bed was scrubbed with disinfectant solution. The whole *Jugendheim* was kept scrupulously clean.

My brother's hair was crawling with lice. He was terribly upset and helpless. I combed his hair with a fine comb to get rid of the eggs. Frequent washing of his hair and rinsing with a vinegar solution finally got this problem under control.

At the beginning of 1943 Sigi Kwasniewski put me in charge of room No. 8. Many of my new charges were orphans. The layout of our room was similar to the room I had shared with Hilde Dublon: three-storey bunk-beds on three walls and a table and benches in the middle of the room. We had a shelf arrangement in the farthest corner of the room close to the window.

My father was always striving to improve our living conditions. He built countless things large and small, including our cupboard which had 30 compartments: one for each girl to store her food rations and eating utensils. This eliminated the storage of food items and containers in the bunk-beds.

We had 'organized' a zinc bathtub and all kinds of cleaning materials. (Most of the furniture and equipment for L414 had been 'organized', which meant that you took what you could get your hands on.) At the beginning of L414 there was not even a bunk-bed available to us. My father 'sleuthed' many wooden boards from the building shed (the *Bauhof*) away from their intended use in the production of coffins. The German word for 'sleuthing' is *geschleust* which has the same meaning as 'organized'. (We used these expressions to convey that we had either stolen or bartered for something – it signified an enormous achievement.)

Some of us occasionally received Red Cross packages. The SS ordered us to write postcards, or, more accurately, to fill in pre-printed cards acknowledging receipt and sometimes even contents. They used this scheme to convince the International Red Cross that all packages were distributed, which of course they were not. They also forced us to write notes like 'We are fine' (*Uns geht es gut*). What better proof that Theresienstadt was a very nice Jewish town to live in!

My father and brother and I received enormous numbers of packages addressed to us individually, bearing numerous fictitious senders' names and posted from different places in Germany. This was the work of my mother and Aunt Minchen. All packages received by me were shared with my girls. My mother sent a lot of vitamins, cookies, hard sausage, sweets, bouillon cubes, crackers, canned meats, canned cheese spreads, etc.

Since many of the packages were posted in Beckum and Hamm in Westphalia, Germany, we knew that my Aunt Minchen, who lived in Lippborg (which was located relatively close to these towns) had been busy bartering and organizing on the black market. We also correctly suspected that my mother lived in Vienna for a time since we also received a fair number of parcels from fictitious senders living in that city.

Polentransporte, Kindertransporte! (Transports to Poland, Children's Transports!) In the winter of 1942/43 people in the ghetto were gripped by panic. The persistent *'bonkes'* (*bonkes* meant rumours) going around told us of impending transports from Theresienstadt to Poland. A lot of children from our Youth Home were put into these transports. The SS spread rumours that the children were all going to Switzerland.

'Poland' was uttered with fear and foreboding. To most of us it meant work camps and cold winters. No sane person was capable of imagining the atrocities and brutalities which in reality awaited these transports. If you were young and healthy the overwhelming conviction was that you could cope no matter what!

Unfortunately, a lot of these rumours had factual foundations because they trickled down from the office of the Judenälteste (Council of Jewish Elders). This was the Jewish elite who were charged by the SS to administer the ghetto. This Council of Elders was formed at the beginning of 1942. We called them the *Prominenten*. The most prestigious members were: Edelstein, Zucker, Eppstein and Murmelstein. These few men of intellectual and leadership background were in daily touch with the SS and they were forced by the SS *Lager Kommandant* (Camp Commander), first Seidl, then Burger and later Rahm, to execute the horrible edicts handed down to them. They were forced to do the Nazis' dirty work. It was their job to make up the lists of who was to be transported to Poland: the numbers were given to them by the SS, they had to fill in the names.

I called my father 'Papi', our name was Lenneberg, so the girls nicknamed him 'Papiberg', and many people only knew him by that name. Every day after work, my father would visit our room and my brother's room and lend a helping hand. My father had developed a great friendship with Louis Lowy, with whom he had meaningful intellectual exchanges. They argued about literature and enjoyed each other's company.

Louis and I became very good friends. He gave me English and French lessons, and broadened my general education. I enjoyed being with him. Louis contracted a terrible eye infection and he had to spend some time in the *Marodenstube* (sickroom). On one of my visits there he told me that he harboured deep and serious feelings for me. I liked Louis very much but I never thought of him romantically. He was my teacher. This revelation was a blow to me, I was not ready for it and felt very bad to lose the relationship I had enjoyed with him. I knew that it would never be the same again, but Louis and I continued to share a life-long friendship.

We had another outbreak of typhus in 1943 and my brother Walter came down with paratyphoid. I was very worried as I remembered the recent death of my friend Hilde Dublon. Fortunately it turned out to be a relatively mild case. Walter was in the hospital for several weeks, but my father 'organized' enough extra food and puddings to bring about his complete recovery.

Dr Freund was a Czech physician who took care of our Youth Home. I still remember him so vividly: he was in his early thirties, very capable, hard-working and devoted to his many patients. He was blond and tall, of athletic build, with great charm. He was so good-looking that we all had a crush on him but, alas he was married!

During one of our cleaning sprees I fell on to the handle of the zinc tub, I hit it so hard that the handle was bent, and, much more seriously, I developed a painful abscess of my coccyx. Dr Freund lanced it and treated it with tampons, packing the wound with cotton, and miraculously it healed without complications. Later he had to remove part of a very painful infected fingernail, which also healed well after much soaking in soapy water.

A short time after the typhoid outbreak some of my girls developed strange symptoms of imbalance, headache and fever. Dr Freund gave them thorough examinations including neurological tests, such as: 'Close your eyes and touch the tip of your nose with your index finger. Walk in a straight line with your eyes closed.' His diagnosis was infectious encephalitis. How does one isolate two infected children in a room of 30? It was an impossible task. The infected girls were not allowed to have physical contact with anybody in the room. We did our best but a few I more came down with the disease anyway. We were constantly giving ourselves the neurological tests during the epidemic and we were very relieved when we could prove to ourselves that we could walk in a straight line and touch the tip of our nose. Fortunately, the epidemic eventually ran its course.

The Freunds had a baby and we could not understand how he, as a doctor, had allowed this pregnancy to occur. Sadly, Dr Freund and his family ended in Auschwitz like most of the other physicians and nurses.

Not long after I took over room No. 8, Trude from Vienna was made co-*Betreuer* by Sigi Kwasniewski (head of the Youth Home). Trude was about twenty. Her dark complexion, curly black hair and her very dark eyes gave her a rather sexy look. Her chin was pointed and she had a low forehead. Large-boned and of average height, she had a thin waist, big hips and heavy legs. She was intelligent, domineering and extremely aggressive. She was not always open and forthright, and the resulting mistrust bothered me immensely. I found it increasingly difficult to share equally the responsibilities of running room No. 8 as was intended, and twice I came close to giving up my position. At times she could be quite charming and then our relationship was good, but she always fell back into her other character.

Trude's parents and her brother Herbert were also in Theresienstadt. Herbert came down with tuberculosis and he spent a considerable time in the hospital. My mother's and my aunt's packages often contained vitamins and we always shared those with Herbert. Trude* married Sigi Kwasniewski early in 1944, and she became an assistant to her husband. I was very happy to have sole responsibility for my girls.

My brother had his bar mitzvah in September 1943. We were all in tears because he read so beautifully and with such

---

*Trude survived the camps. I was told that Sigi Kwasniewski was shot and killed in a bed of an infirmary barrack by SS guards shortly before the Russian army liberated Auschwitz.

confidence from the Torah. The persecution made us feel our Jewishness most deeply, despite the fact that religious ceremony meant little to my father to the end of his life. We were sad that my mother could not be with us, and we were sad because it took place in Theresienstadt.

My father always cheered us up when gloominess and desperation took hold. He was our anchor, and never once showed a trace of depression. He kept us healthy with his iron determination to survive and to be reunited with my mother. We at least knew that she was alive as we recognized her handwriting on the packages which we were still receiving. Of course, she never used her name or her address.

My friends and fellow youth leaders created a good social and intellectual atmosphere, I enjoyed the discussions and their company. Many of our young people were Zionists, and their goal was to go to Palestine after liberation. They were seriously preparing themselves by studying Ivrith (modern Hebrew). Many wanted to work in agriculture on a kibbutz.

I had a very full schedule: English courses with Dr Klein, French with Louis Lowy, reading with my brother Walter, attending lectures by Dr Eppstein, Engineer Zucker, Dr Beck and Dr Murmelstein. However, my efforts to learn to read music were, unfortunately, not very successful.

We built a stage in the attic of our Youth Home, and produced operas and plays. My brother sang in the children's choir of *Carmen*. Many of our young people acted in plays such as *Maria Stuart*, *The Jews* (Lessing), *The Imagined Invalid* (*Der eingebildete Kranke*), the operas *Brundibar* and *Turandot*, concerts and much more besides. Some plays were written by our young people. A number of our children painted and sketched, and a few of them showed real talent. I still marvel at the energy and creativity so many of us mustered under these most adverse conditions. I become very sad when I am reminded that most of these talented youngsters, who had the courage and initiative to be creative in spite of everything, were finally murdered in Auschwitz.

We endured a time when the entire town was infested with bed bugs, and we at the Youth Home of L414 did not escape this plague. Practically everybody in the ghetto was sleeping in the street. One just could not stand it inside the houses. Our barrack was disinfected and we had to live in the attic. My father helped us to get settled again after the fumes had dissipated. Ultimately we received the plaque for the cleanest, most beautiful *Heim* (home) from the Inspection Commission, which had been created by the Jewish Elders to prevent a recurrence of the scourge we had suffered.

11 · Theresienstadt (2)

The worst day we spent in Theresienstadt, one that will always stick in my memory, was 9 November 1943. It was a damp, depressing cold November day. At about 8 a.m. the SS, under SS Commandant Burger, directed the Jewish Elders immediately to empty the buildings of the entire town. All the inhabitants of Theresienstadt, approximately 38,000 of us spilled into the streets, which were so congested with humanity, young and old, that we could hardly move. The SS, some on horseback, were shouting and screaming with their weapons drawn. They forced us to move out of the ghetto until we all spilled into the Bauschowitz Basin – a large flat area, that in times past had presumably been used as a parade ground – to be counted. We heard shots from the direction of the prison called the Little Fortress (*die kleine Festung*). The basin was surrounded by hilly terrain, and SS with automatic weapons were stationed on the surrounding hills, in addition to armed soldiers on horseback.

I was holding onto my brother. I was sure that. we would be slaughtered. This was how the Germans counted close to 40,000 people. Old and young, men and women and children, babies – everybody had to stand in formation and woe to those who did not follow orders, as they would feel the butt of an SS rifle or the force of a leather whip.

This so-called counting went on for hours. It was getting colder and it had started to rain. Many old people and children collapsed under the constant screaming and cursing by the SS, interrupted only by recurring gunshots from the Little Fortress. There was no drink or food or blankets or shelter. I felt cold and wet and numb. It was already dark when the SS finally disappeared, and we were herded back into the ghetto, all 38,000 of us, totally soaked from the still-falling rain. (Some people did not get back until the middle of the night.)

A number of rooms in our barrack had been searched while we were being counted. They (supposedly) found some money or valuables and they arrested somebody. A substantial number of people died during and after the census, and the toll was especially heavy among the elderly. On that night many people lost their lives in the much-feared *'kleine Festung'* – few ever came out of it alive anyway.

Commandant Burger accused the Jewish Elders of falsifying the camp records. He particularly singled out Jacob Edelstein, he also accused him of having ridden his bicycle beyond the limits of the ghetto. Edelstein and his family were subsequently sent to Auschwitz to be gassed.

Many people in the ghetto did not place the same trust in Dr Murmelstein as they did in his fellow Elders. I believe that Dr Murmelstein was the only one of the original Jewish Elders who remained in Theresienstadt and survived.

The beginning of 1944 brought more notifications for transports to 'Work Camps', and one day I happened to be with my father in his room when the house elder (*Hausälteste*), the person responsible for the people in the building, in which he also lived, handed him a piece of paper. It had my father's name on it, with the directive to appear at the collection point for the next transport. It is difficult to convey the worry, apprehension and feeling of helplessness and ultimately resignation which I felt at that moment. This transport was made up of strong and healthy men only. He spent about 14 weeks in the KZ work camp (*Arbeitslager*) Zossen, near Berlin, as part of the crew which built Hitler's bunker. They were treated horribly by the guards. They had to work from 5 a.m. until late in the evening, but in spite of that he returned to Theresienstadt healthy and fit.

While my father was in Zossen, I developed vague symptoms and a swollen liver. Rest in the sick-bay (*Marodenstube*) restored my health. A short time later a painful infected tooth had to be extracted.

On 24 April 1944 I celebrated my birthday among the girls, my friends, and most especially, my father and brother. The girls had been preparing a surprise birthday party for me. They had worked very hard and very thoughtfully. They presented me with a play they had written and carefully rehearsed. I received so many meaningful presents, like poems and small things which they had been able somehow to obtain or make themselves. The best gift was a package and card with my mother's handwriting. My brother Walter gave me several gifts which he had carefully wrapped and addressed 'To my dear sister'. I can still see the table with all these expressions of love and caring and gratitude, particularly from the girls.

In the spring of 1944 SS Kommandant Rahm who had succeeded Kommandant Burger, announced that Theresienstadt was going to undergo 'Beautification' (*Stadtverschönerung*). The preparations for his plans lasted for many weeks: houses were painted, everything, including pavements, was scrubbed. Flowers and trees were planted, patches of dirt were covered with grass-seed. A new pavilion was built to accommodate the newly formed band (*Kurkapelle*). Streets were renamed, the 'L' and 'Q' being replaced with 'Seestrasse', 'Rathausgasse', 'Gartenstrasse' and so on, (L414, our Youth Home, became Hauptstrasse 14.)

A bank was opened, ghetto money was printed in 'Czech Kronen' with a Star of David (*Magen David*) on one side of the paper money and a picture of Moses with his stone plates bearing the ten commandments on the other side, it was printed in several denominations. A library was opened. Stores were established, decorated and filled with items confiscated from the luggage of newly arrived transports. Grocery stores displayed food and sweets. There was a barber shop and a beauty parlour. One of the buildings was designated as the new theatre.

A terrace was created with garden tables and chairs complete with umbrellas. The tables were decorated with fresh flowers. A menu was printed and posted. Uniformed waitresses were serving ice cream, lemonade and coffee. The band played.

Children were playing near the pavilion. A children's choir was singing. Only well-dressed and good-looking people were allowed in the streets. Old or 'ugly' Jews were forbidden to go outside (*Ausgangsverbot*).

The SS Commander himself walked through the streets of the ghetto and visited the fake cafés and stores. When he saw an old or dishevelled-looking person he ordered them off the streets, and he made sure the ghetto did not look crowded. A transport had left Theresienstadt only a few days before 'beautification' commenced, obviously to help present the image that this was an uncrowded city were Jews enjoyed every privilege imaginable.

Suddenly we lived in a Jewish town under Jewish control with a Jewish band and Jewish paper money. The Jewish Elder was now a mayor. Some of our young people who had to participate in this make-believe told us that they saw our 'new mayor' decked out in a meticulously tailored suit decorated with a gold watch on a long gold chain sharing the SS limousine with the important foreign dignitaries.

The whole ghetto was a temporary stage, precisely organized in preparation for the arrival of the Red Cross inspection delegation. The Germans had put up this charade to convince them, that in spite of rumours to the contrary, the Jews were well treated in the ghettos and concentration camps. The drama played for a very short time only: it was filmed and we were the actors.

Herr Rahm's efforts were quite successful. The members of the Red Cross never asked to see the inside of the overcrowded barracks which housed the old and dying. They never asked to speak privately to any of the prisoners. They bought this hoax lock, stock and barrel.

Kommandant Rahm was still basking in all his accomplishments even after the Red Cross visitors had left. He ordered the famous actor Kurt Gerron, who was caught by the Gestapo in Holland and then deported to Theresienstadt, to make a film of this mirage with the title *Der Führer schenkt den Juden eine Stadt* (the Führer gives a city to the Jews as a gift). I can still see Kurt Gerron busily directing his camera crew in the streets of the ghetto. Shortly after the film was completed, he was put into a transport to Auschwitz where he perished in the gas chamber.

12 · Auschwitz

On 2 June 1944 we celebrated my father's forty-fifth birthday. Even though he tried to hide it from us we knew that he missed my mother dreadfully.

So many transports were leaving Theresienstadt. We were living in fear whenever a list came out and notifications were distributed, and then we were relieved when we were not on that list. These emotions of fear and relief became more and more our way of life. Many of us realized that we would end up in Poland sooner or later. Although Poland still meant work camps to us, this atmosphere influenced our mood on my brother's birthday on 23 September 1944. We all felt subdued even though each one of us tried to hide it from the other. I had a sense of foreboding and it was not good.

On 24 September an announcement was made that 5,000 men aged sixteen to sixty would be transported to Königstein near Dresden into a work camp. One of the Elders, Otto Zucker (an engineer by profession and thus still addressed as Herr Ingenieur) was named transport leader. The men were processed for this transport in one of the barracks (Hamburger Kaserne). This process was referred to as being sluiced (*geschleust*). Many of us spent day and night in the Hamburger *Schleuse* (sluice) with our departing friends. We brought as much food to them as we were able to 'organize'. After this transport had left there was a general feeling of quiet panic in the ghetto. We felt paralysed.

On 30 September 1944, I was visiting my father in his room when the building Elder entered and handed him a slip of paper with his name on it, ordering him into the next transport. This was a terrible blow, but I had had a premonition that our days in Theresienstadt were numbered. The only difference with this transport was that 500 women were allowed to 'volunteer' to accompany their men, thereby allowing families to stay together.

I have often wondered whether these different edicts and rules on how a transport was constituted was in effect a game the SS played for their own amusement. It really did not matter whether they allowed men or women, or both, with or without children, into a transport since I am sure they knew that the destination was Auschwitz.

I, of course, believed that we would end up in another labour camp, especially since my father had spent some three and a half months in Zossen, and he had returned to Theresienstadt. I also felt very strongly that we should keep our family together. That after all was the reason my father and my brother had volunteered to go with me to Theresienstadt. My father was very much against our joining him on this transport. After a lot of disputing and arguing I finally won his approval because I probably correctly reasoned that we would be in a transport very soon anyway, so why not stay together. I persuaded him that this way we had a better chance to survive.

On 1 October 1944, we were driven to the train under the lashes and the swinging whip of SS Officer Heindl. Except for one or two passenger carriages, the rest of the train was made up of cattle trucks. My father, my brother and I were pushed into a passenger carriage. Rumour had it that the destination was Königstein, a small town approximately 20 miles southeast of Dresden. We believed that we were going to a labour camp there, within Germany, and not to one of the feared Polish camps, but my feelings were not good. Our *Junge* ('our boy' was an expression I used whenever as I referred to my brother) was very subdued. I believe he also had a sense of foreboding that nothing good was awaiting us where we were going.

Since it was Yom Kippur, some people in our carriage, like Herr Jakob, the secretary of our Youth Home L414, even refused to eat the meagre rations the SS had allowed for our trip.

We did not know which route the train was taking. My father and a number of the other men in our compartment took careful note of each station we passed. Someone said: 'We just passed Dresden!' The train moved on and on. Somebody else declared: 'We are not going to Königstein, we are much too far east by now!' One of our fellow prisoners wondered whether our destination could be Birkenau, he asked my father for his opinion. My father did not answer, he just looked ashen. I asked him whether he thought that we were going to Birkenau. He shook his head, but from then on he never spoke again. I had never heard the name 'Birkenau' before, I did not know what it meant, but I am sure that my father knew. He had probably heard of the existence of these camps when he worked on the bunker in Berlin, as he would have had contact with prisoners from other concentration camps. He never mentioned anything to us after his return to Theresienstadt, but it was nevertheless clear to me then that he was holding things back from us.

We were apprehensively watching the station signs as our train moved on. We were already in Poland. Nobody uttered a word. The people's faces around us looked pale and drained, premonition and fear showed in their eyes. The train stopped. People around me were gripped by a silent panic, unable to utter a word.

It was 3 October 1944. We had arrived in Auschwitz. The name 'Auschwitz' did not mean any more to me than Birkenau. (In fact Auschwitz is the German name for Oswiecim, a Polish town 30 miles west of Cracow.)

The train doors were opened. Tall, uniformed SS in shining leather boots screamed at us: 'Leave all luggage in the cars! Get out! Quickly, hurry up!' (*Raus, schnell, schnell, schneller!*) They enforced their barking and screaming with their whips and drawn guns. Vicious German shepherd dogs were held by some SS men on short leashes. The dogs were straining to get at us. The SS showered us with vile vulgar insults, they kept shouting commands at us. 'Women this way! Men that way! Line up in fives!' Prisoners in striped prison uniforms were moving swiftly into the carriages to unload the luggage following orders and commands the SS were barking at them. I followed the herds of women. I obeyed the instructions. I felt nothing: I was numb. I looked over to where the men were forming large columns, and tried to get a glimpse of my father and my brother, but I could not see them anymore.

In front of us lay a huge complex of camps as far as the eye could see. Each camp (*Lager*) had many primitively built barracks. Each camp was separated from the next adjacent camp by approximately ten-foot high electrically charged fencing. All these camps were mired in grey mud. Each camp housed thousands of human beings. It was a grey, damp overcast October day. We walked through the greyish-brown sludge; there was no tree, not one blade of grass, not even a weed, nothing was growing in this bleak wasteland.

First the men marched away, five abreast. Then the women were ordered to march forward in the same formation. We all had to walk past a tall SS officer, wearing grey suede gloves on his outstretched hands. He pointed into the direction which each one of us had to follow. We learned a bit later that the SS officer was Dr Mengele, who made the selection from each arriving transport as to who would live and who would die. If he pointed to the right it meant work, if he pointed to the left it meant into the gas. It seemed that the selection was often quite arbitrary. Sometimes older people were allowed to live a little longer, and often younger people were condemned to die in the gas chamber. I learned from 'old' inmates that the officers of the SS drank frequently, and that affected their mood and consequently the prisoners' chances of, in many cases only temporary, survival.

Dr Mengele looked at me and pointed to the right. It was raining. We walked through the thick mud constantly being screamed at by the young SS men walking along both sides of our newly formed column. Many were not more than seventeen or eighteen. The SS and their dogs were continually forcing us to move on, screaming at us, 'Faster, faster!' Our column wound its way between the electric fences of one camp after another. When a transport had arrived no person was allowed outside the barrack. They called that '*Blocksperre*' (lock-up). A woman in one of the camps which we were passing was outside her barrack very close to the electric fence. She recognized someone in our column and called out to her. The SS guard fairly close to me screamed at her, 'Woman if you don't go inside I'll shoot you!'

(*Weib wenn Du nich rein gehst – knalle ich dich nieder!*),
Immediately he pulled out his gun and fired it at her. The
woman cried out and fell into the mud, blood pooling around
her. I had never before seen a human being murdered. That
was my introduction to Auschwitz, and I whispered to myself:
'You'll never get out of here alive.'

Our column stopped at a large stone barrack called 'Sauna'.
We were pushed into a huge room where we had to strip
completely naked before the staring young SS men who were
sneering at and insulting us. Prisoners shaved the hair off our
heads and bodies. Even though we were naked and hairless
they searched our bodies for valuables. We were repeatedly
being warned of the consequences if we tried to hide
anything in the crevices of our bodies. The whole procedure
was a model of an efficient assembly line. I followed orders
quickly and I tried not to attract attention by stepping out of
line. I looked at my shaven, naked dehumanized fellow
prisoners and I did not yet fully comprehend that I was part
of this ugly-looking humanity.

Next we were shoved into a large room with shower heads
protruding from the ceiling. Ice-cold water drenched our
frozen, naked bodies briefly. There was no soap or towel to
dry ourselves with. Several women near me were given lashes
on their wet bodies with a swinging leather whip by a woman
guard because they were not moving fast enough.

We had no names and no numbers. So many transports
were arriving daily in Auschwitz at that time that they had
given up tattooing prisoners. They gave each of us a dirty
cotton dress and wooden clogs. This was all accomplished in
record time under the scornful gazes and shouts of '*Schneller!
Schneller!*' by the guards. A prisoner with a large pot of red
paint smeared a long glossy stripe down the back of our
dresses before we were pushed out into the muddy road
again. It was cold and drizzling with rain.

Both Auschwitz and Birkenau were part of the greater
Auschwitz concentration camp complex. We were herded into
Camp C in Birkenau, and then into one of the low barracks.
These barracks had rows and rows of three-tier plank beds,

and a dirt floor. There were no windows. Our barrack was so overcrowded that we were squeezed together on the plank in a locked position, unable to turn, unless everybody on the plank turned at the same time. Each plank had one dirty clammy blanket.

Each barrack had a barrack elder (*Blockälteste*), a prisoner with a privileged position and a distinctive mark on her dress. There was a whole hierarchy of inmates with special positions. The most feared were the '*Kapos*', the camp police. Many of these inmates, some Jewish and some non-Jewish, were collaborating with the SS. Many did so willingly, and some were just as cruel as the SS and readily did their dirty work. Some were probably so dehumanized from long stays in the camp, seeing people being murdered and gassed daily, that they would do anything to enhance their chances of survival.

If one of us tried to get off the plank without being commanded to do so, the *Blockälteste* was ready to flog them with her switch. Our food was brought into the camp by male inmates. It was then dished out into pots. One pot for each plank. We had to eat this indefinable thin mush with our hands as we had no spoons. The hands of everybody on the plank tried to get as much food out of the pot as fast as ten fingers could lift it.

We heard some screaming during the night. Somewhere in our barrack, the women on one of the top planks fell on those below them. We even got used to the constant yelling as our senses became dulled. We were not able to wash ourselves. We could use the latrine only when the whole barrack was led to it. That happened once or twice in 24 hours.

The first evening when we were led to the latrine, we saw flames leaping about 600 feet into the blood-red sky: the chimneys were spewing their burning cinders. Inmates who had been in the camp longer than we, the new arrivals, told us in wailing tones: 'The gas chambers and crematoria are working overtime, transports must have arrived again.' I saw the red sky, I saw the large smoke stacks spewing red-hot cinders. We could all smell it, but I could not admit to myself that it could be so.

The latrine was a very large cesspool with long wooden

planks forming a rectangle around it. The planks were covered with faces. We had to sit on these planks or we would feel the switch across our back. Prisoners who were obviously ill with dysentery or paratyphoid were dragging themselves along, some with high fever; nobody dared to report sick. To be sick meant death in the gas chamber. Even at this stage the fear of death was overwhelming, most wanted to live. Almost every day, however, somebody in our camp threw herself against the electric wire and was instantly electrocuted.

One morning as we were leaving our barrack to go to the latrine, I saw a truck in our camp. Male prisoners were picking up some bodies of women who had died, including one who had thrown herself against the electric wire. I recognized one of the men, and he recognized me. I knew Inge and Hermann Hirschfeld* from Theresienstadt. They had both been part of our transport, Inge and I were in the barrack in Camp C. Hermann had somehow succeeded in making contact with his wife Inge while he was picking up the dead bodies. He also whispered to her that my father and brother never made it into the camp. I knew then that I would never see my father and my brother again. I felt that they were dead. For the rest of my stay in the camps I never had any more hope that they had survived.

Twice a day the whole C Camp had to assemble outside for inspection and to be counted, no matter what the weather. We had to stand in formation for two to three hours. The SS, particularly some of the women guards would hit us with rubber clubs screaming profanities at us: 'Will you stand still you pregnant lice!' (*Ihr schwangeren Filzläuse*) was their favourite manner of addressing us. Their vulgar language and their insane outbursts and screaming while perpetrating one sadistic act after another on the prisoners was beyond the capacity of a normal human being to comprehend, but I became desensitized. I was standing at roll-call, but my mind, my senses, my feelings had retracted into a cocoon. The November chill and moisture penetrated our thinly clad bodies and bare scalp but somehow even the ability to feel the cold became dulled.

*Both Inge and Hermann Hirschfeld survived the camps.

A few times a week during this month of November women were selected for work by the SS. This selection was made outside the barrack. The inmates were ordered to strip naked and then walk past the glaring SS in single file. The SS men exchanged coarse jokes and made mocking gestures toward the naked women, while their German shepherd dogs strained at the leash and barked. The prisoners were paralysed with fear. Everybody wanted to be selected for work, as work meant life. Representatives of some of the largest German industries often helped in that selection.

Some prisoners, because of the work they had been assigned to, moved from one camp to another within the larger Auschwitz complex. They heard the whispers about the inner workings of the camp, which transports went into the gas and which were allowed to live. From them we learned the name of Dr Mengele, they also knew the names of the worst guards and *Kapos*.

Prisoners who had been in the camp for any length of time looked like skeletons* covered with grey, lifeless, wrinkled skin. They had hollow eyes and haunted expressions of fear in their faces. Their hair had started to sprout again. They were dirty and infested with lice. I could not look at them but I sometimes wondered how long I would survive there, and whether in time I would look just like them.

There was also frequent selection for the gas chambers in all camps in Auschwitz and Birkenau. Whenever selection was taking place, no prisoner was allowed to leave the barrack. The SS enforced what was called '*Blocksperre*' (lock-up). They applied every precaution to prevent anybody from escaping. Since most of the prisoners in these selections had been in Auschwitz for many months, and since almost all of them were walking skeletons, many of them very sick, they knew that they would not be selected for work. If there was ever any outbreak of panic it was among these people. They were quickly held in check when the dogs were let loose on them. There was a particularly vicious woman guard who was always present at any selection or search for somebody unaccounted for. She was about forty, short, with a leather

*Inmates referred to these emaciated creatures as '*Muselmänner*'.

whip in her hand, holding a straining German shepherd dog on a short leash. Her very appearance filled us with terror.

A lot of Hungarian girls were housed in some of the other barracks of C camp, they were probably 14 to 17 years old. They had already been there for a relatively long time. (Survival in Auschwitz was measured in weeks and months.) They were emaciated and sick, and they knew too well what their selection meant. Several of these young girls tried to escape to another barrack where no selection was taking place because officials there were too occupied with new arrivals, as ours were. A few prisoners ran into our barrack to save themselves. The SS shot at them from all sides. We heard heart-wrenching cries of mortal terror. We did not know what was going on. We were sure that they would shoot all of us. The shooting finally subsided. The SS had left our camp.

One girl had managed to hide in our barrack. It was obvious that the *Blockälteste* knew her. This poor emaciated girl, who looked more like a wild animal than a human being, told us that she had been in Auschwitz for a long time and that she had escaped many selections. There was an almost insane look in her eyes. She told us that the SS officer who did all the selecting was 'Dr Mengele', and that he also did medical experiments on inmates and awful operations, and when these young women, who were his guinea pigs, were of no use to him anymore, he would send them to the gas chambers. She further told us that one girl she knew had survived so far because one of the SS was using her, that he gave her food and clothing. She told us how sadistic an older, short woman guard was, that she would not hesitate to let her dog maul an inmate. We listened and looked at her in disbelief. She was there, she was giving testimony here in this barrack in the most forsaken spot on this planet, yet somehow it all seemed to be happening far from me even though I was part of it. I turned more and more inward, insulating myself, and so I preserved some strength and kept my sanity.

After weeks at C Camp, interrupted only by roll-calls and inspection, I was wondering if we would ever be assigned to work. Then one day we were paraded in front of several SS officers and one civilian, obviously a representative of industry. We felt their gazes, their eyes were sweeping over our naked bodies from head to toe, evaluating each one of us as to our fitness to work. The civilian asked me to show him my hands. The *Kapo* barked at us to get dressed quickly, and before I knew what was happening, I and a small group of women were pushed out of the barrack. The *Kapo* screamed, 'Start marching, *schneller, schneller!*' – she then led us to a building which had a sign '*Sauna*' on it.

By that time we had been in Auschwitz long enough to fear the shower heads of the *Sauna* (bath); we had learned in C Camp that the gas chambers were also equipped with shower heads. We were ordered to strip naked and leave our clothes outside before entering, I interpreted that as a bad sign – why did they not allow us to bring our clothes into the building? Was it because we would not need them any more? I looked suspiciously at the shower heads protruding from the ceiling, and then we felt the ice cold water trickling down our bodies. We were so relieved – maybe we really had a chance to make it after all. I was given a clean cotton dress, a black coat and a pair of leather shoes which miraculously fitted my feet – some of the other girls were not so lucky. We were so hopeful, but we soon became very concerned again when we ended up in the women's concentration camp (*Frauen Konzentrations Lager* or *FKL*) in Birkenau.

We were now mostly among non-Jews. The inmates here wore distinguishing signs: Jews had a star, Gentiles wore different coloured triangles or other markings on their clothing which identified them as, for example, murderers, other criminals or political prisoners. Our barrack had an abundance of murderers including the *Blockälteste*, who was feared for her brutality and beatings. She put me into latrine service (*Latrinendienst*). We had to carry the huge pails filled with urine and faeces and carry them to the latrines at night. We were accompanied on that trip by a *Kapo*. The prisoners of the barrack were led to the latrines only during daylight hours. on these trips we would stare at the sky again, unable to comprehend that the burning sky reflected the burnt particles of our people and we were the potential fodder of this inferno.

The food was better in this camp. The prisoners were healthier and the barrack was much cleaner and less crowded. The planks were covered with straw mattresses and each of us was assigned a plank bed. Zdena (or Zdenka) Glickova from Pilsen, Czechoslovakia, and Hilde Buschhoff (Buschi) from Holland were given planks next to me. Buschi and Zdena and I almost instantly formed a bond. I cannot recall how long we stayed at *FKL*. Time became abstract. The crimson, searing skies and the smell of burning flesh were with us all the time.

13 · Rejection in Kudowa

There came a day, probably in the middle or at the end of December 1944 (I have to say probably because we had no conception of time, days of the week, dates, or even what month we lived in), when we were told to hurry up and form a column: *'Schneller, Schneller – Auf Transport!'* (into a transport). We marched to the railway siding and about 50 of us were pushed into a cattle truck. We spent one whole day and night crammed into the tightly bolted damp, cold cattle truck without food or drink. We had no idea where we were heading – there was not even a tiny slit or crack in the wooden plank walls of the truck through which we could get a glimpse of the outside.

I sat in one corner of that truck, and the many weeks in Auschwitz passed in front of my eyes. I saw the electrified barbed-wire fences, the manned towers with machine guns, the fire-spewing crematoria, the brutal faces of the guards, the straining dogs, the woman who was shot in front of my eyes and who was lying in her own blood. I saw the emaciated Hungarian girl who had sought cover in our barrack. I wondered: 'What is next, where will we end up?'

The train stopped, the door was opened and we read the station sign: 'Bad Kudowa-Sackisch' (now in Polish, it is Kudowa-Zdroj). I had never heard that name before. This town is situated in the Glatz region of the Sudeten Mountains (Glatzer Bergland; Glatz is now Polish and is called Klodzko). We must have travelled about 180 miles in a westerly direction since leaving Auschwitz. SS guards led us into a camp near what we were told was an aeroplane factory. We were housed in what seemed to us luxurious dormitories.

The next morning all new arrivals had to assemble on the grounds outside the dormitories to be inspected by an official of the factory. His eyes wandered quickly down the assembled line, and he called out: 'Everybody who wears spectacles step forward!' Buschi (Hilde Buschhoff) was standing next to me. I started to pull my glasses off with the intention of hiding them, but Buschi whispered to me, 'Leave your glasses on – have we not gambled with our fate enough?' (*Haben wir nicht genug Schicksal gespielt?*)

(Buschi was making reference to her decision to join her husband when the SS put him into a transport in Amsterdam even though he was not Jewish. They were seeing off their Jewish friends who had been designated for deportation. An SS man had screamed at him then: 'If you are such a Jew-lover, you can join them!' and he forced him into the transport. I had mentioned to Buschi earlier that my father and my brother had volunteered to join me when I was sent to Theresienstadt, and then my brother and I had decided to go with my father to a 'work camp' and we ended up in Auschwitz.)

I immediately put my glasses back on and I stepped out of line. Zdena also wore glasses and she also had to step forward. Buschi was asked to step forward even though she did not wear glasses. Six of us were rejects, he called us 'Useless Scum' (*Ausschuss*), and we were separated from the workers who were allowed to stay in Kudowa.

I said to Buschi, 'Why did they select you, you don't wear glasses?', and I can still hear her reply: 'Fate, Uschi, it's destined to be that way!' (*Schicksal, Uschi, es soll so sein!*). We were going to be shipped back to Auschwitz as 'unfit for work' (*nicht arbeitsfähig*), and that meant into the gas chambers. We saw a large group of sick women waiting in the courtyard: they had been replaced by workers from our transport, and we, the six rejects, had to join them.

A female guard took charge of us who seemed more humane: she did not scream at us, nor did she use foul language. I pleaded with her to let me stay in Kudowa. I tried to convince her that I was healthy and a good hard worker. I finally told her that I was not really Jewish, that my mother was Aryan, that we were German. She assured me with some sympathy that she could not help me: 'there is nothing I can do!' (*ich kann aber doch nichts tun!*). I have always felt badly that stooped to that level of pleading for my life. I think it is the only time during my almost three years of imprisonment that I was ashamed of my conduct.

We were led to the railway tracks, where the very large group of desperately sick Hungarian women suffering from all kinds of ailments were already waiting. The guards assigned to them were starting to load them into the cattle truck of the huge transport train. Many had open sores on their swollen legs: they were suffering from impetigo and other horrible infections. They were a pitiful sight to behold. It scared me to look at them because they mirrored what would inevitably happen to each of us.

The six of us were told to board the last empty cattle truck. Two German soldiers, not SS, were guarding us. One was middle-aged, while the second one seemed very young to me. The door was closed and the train started to move. Of course, the truck had no windows and no crack was discernible through which we could get a glimpse as to which direction the train was going. We were given no food or drink. One bucket in the corner of the truck served as our toilet.

Beside Zdena and Buschi and myself, the three other women who shared the truck with us were Hannah Kohorn from Karlsbad, Anka Konigova from Prague and Hilde Sonnenberg from Germany. All six of us spoke German. We shared our background, our experiences and our fears. All of us knew that we would be gassed upon our return to Auschwitz. Even though the Red Army was rapidly advancing into that part of Poland, transports were still arriving in Auschwitz at the beginning of January. Even after the liberation of Auschwitz on 27 January 1945, other German concentration camps such as Gross-Rosen, located in Silesia, were still functioning – the lives of those poor Hungarian women most likely ended there.

All of us had been in Theresienstadt before being transported to Auschwitz. The soldiers listened to our conversations; they exchanged concerned glances and they showed sympathy and consideration. They tried to give us privacy when we used the bucket. They gave us some of their bread and cheese. The younger soldier seemed quite upset and at times close to tears. He could not comprehend that his people did things like that. I remember him saying: 'I'd rather be dead' (*Da bin ich lieber tot*).

We must have presented a pretty awful picture to them, with our hair shaven off, totally unkempt and dressed in ill-fitting rags. They overheard our desperate talk of our fears and acceptance of the fate awaiting us upon our return to Auschwitz. Buschi and I were discussing the possibility of throwing ourselves against one of the high-tension wire fences: we thought that preferable to death in the gas chamber. We were holding counsel, but we had no options: we were trapped. The soldiers heard it all as we spoke their language.

14 · *Merzdorf Labour Camp*

After two days in the cattle truck our train stopped. The two soldiers opened the door. I saw a sign which said: 'Merzdorf/Riesengebirge'. We all gave a sigh of relief, 'This is Merzdorf not Auschwitz!' Merzdorf is a village near Landeshut in the Sudeten mountains of Silesia in a mountain chain called Riesengebirge (now Polish, Marciszow). We had probably travelled close to 75 miles in a north-westerly direction since leaving Kudowa.

The soldiers told us to jump out of the truck and follow them. There were no SS on the platform. We felt the stares of the local people as the two soldiers led us, six filthy-looking women, hair shorn off, dressed in tatters, through the main street of the village and then to a large factory complex, and ultimately delivered us to the female commander of a very large work camp: a big, brutal-looking woman, who wanted to send us back to Auschwitz. They exchanged some words with her in the factory yard, clicked their heels, then gave a military Hitler salute and left immediately through the gate without looking back at us.

Thus two German soldiers saved six German-speaking Jewish prisoners from certain death. I have tried, unsuccessfully, to find an answer as to why our lives were spared: why were we six put in one cattle truck with two German soldiers while the sick Hungarian women were packed tightly into trucks with no room to spare? After all, the factory foreman in Kudowa had rejected us for work, he had called us 'useless scum' (*Ausschuss*). Did the woman guard in Kudowa speak to the soldiers? Undoubtedly, my questions will never be answered.

We realized that we were in some sort of factory, but we had no idea what exactly they were manufacturing. We were led into a building and climbed the stairs to the third floor. The prisoners who worked for Kramsta, Mettner & Frahne lived in a very large room with rows and rows of tiered bunk-beds. We were led into a spacious shower room where we took hot showers. We were each given a towel. We had not seen a towel or felt hot water on our bodies since we left Theresienstadt, and we were totally overwhelmed by the civilized treatment we were receiving. All six of us were moved to tears after coming out of sheer hell. We were also each given a kerchief, an apron and wooden clogs and a blanket with our new number stitched into it. I became No. 67269. We were assigned six bunks with thin straw mattresses adjacent to each other. We shared every crumb of extra food. We supported, protected, encouraged, worried and truly cared about each other. I was a lot younger than my five friends who called me '*Das Kind*'* (the child). We became a very close knit family.

I was assigned to 'transport' work, as were Buschi and Zdena. Hannah, Hanka and Hilde had to work in the factory. Kramsta, Mettner & Frahne was a textile mill. The operation started with the arrival of the rail freight trucks loaded with large bundles of flax plants. The raw flax was processed into fragile yarn. In the spinnery it was twisted into thread. Ultimately, huge looms wove the thread into linen cloth.

Most of the approximately 450 prisoners were Polish and Hungarian Jews. The Poles had been in Merzdorf the longest and they held all the good jobs. All the cooks and kitchen personnel were Polish. The tall, fat, vulgar and cruel Erna Rinke was the much-feared commander of our camp (*Frau Kommandantin*). The Polish Jewish Camp Elder (*Lagerälteste*) was the coarse, common Bronya, screaming commands at us in her harsh, heavily accented mispronounced German laced with vulgar expletives. Bronya was of medium height, with a fat face and cropped blonde hair. She wore good boots and warm clothing. One often heard her uncouth loud laughter when she was talking to the Nazi guards or even to the commandant. She was the most enthusiastic tool of *Frau Kommandantin*.

*Buschi referred to me as '*Das Kind*' until her death, and to Hannah I am still '*Das Kind*'.

The job of the recording secretary (*die Schreiberin*) was held by a German-Jewish prisoner: a low-key, educated woman who was responsible for keeping records and taking care of the office and secretarial work for the commandant. She was always present when we were counted.

Bronya would wake us at 5 a.m. screaming, 'Off the beds, out, roll-call!' (*Von de* [sic] *Betten, raus, Appell!*). 'Faster, faster, faster!' (*Schneller, schneller, schneller!*). We had to assemble in the large cobble-stone yard which was encircled by factory buildings and closed off by a huge gate. We stood to attention in cold winter weather, often for an hour or longer, to be counted. We did not have underwear or socks or warm winter clothing to protect us. After the counting had finished, Bronya would assume a military pose and report in her grammatically incorrect German: '*Frau Kommandantin*' (if the commandant was present) or '*Frau Aufseherin*' (if a female Nazi guard was in charge), 'I report 380 prisoners present, 80 at work' (*Frau Kommandantin, Ichch melde* [sic] *380 Häftlinge zu Appell angetreten, 80 bei die* [sic] *Arbeit!*).

Following the early morning counting we got a small ration of bread and black chicory water called coffee. After that every prisoner joined her work group (*Arbeitskolonne*). Each group had a group leader (*Kolonnenführerin*). Our group leader was a Polish-Jewish young woman named Bronka. Bronka was tall, well-built, a bit of a vulgar beauty. She wore very warm, good and stylish winter clothing, including a heavy woollen winter coat and sturdy leather boots. She was one of the privileged clique and showed no feeling for us.

She was accountable for each one of us to the Nazi guard who accompanied us to our work. It was Bronka's responsibility to check that the same number of workers were at all times at the work-sites, and that the number leaving the camp was the same as the number returning. She had to accompany us to the toilet and return us to our work group. When we had to go to the toilet we had to approach the Nazi guard, stand at attention and address her: '*Frau Aufseherin, ich melde mich zur Toilette*' (Madam Prison Guard, I report for the toilet). On our return, we would have to say: '*Frau Aufseherin ich melde mich zurück*' (Madam Prison Guard, I report back).

Except for a few German foremen who had to be addressed as '*Herr Meister*', most of the workers were women prisoners. There were two Belgian, one French and a few other war prisoners working in the factory as well. Work in the 'Transport' was very heavy men's work. We had to unload the flax from the freight trucks at the railway siding onto flat-bed wagons. We learned to load evenly so that the wagon would not tip over. We were also the horses: two of us would grab the handle, while several more would push the rear of the vehicle. In this way we drove and shoved and pulled the wagons to the unloading deck of the factory warehouse. Often they were so heavily loaded that a number of us had to pull at the handle of the front shaft while the others pushed the rear and the sides of the wagon to make it move at all.

We were afraid to upset the *Herr Meister* who had a bad temper: he would become particularly mean and nasty when things did not go well. We worked hard, used our heads and our best judgement, and became quite skilled as we wanted to keep our jobs. The hardest and dirtiest work was unloading the coal trucks. Whenever freight trains arrived we had to work until every truck was unloaded and every wagon pulled back to the factory.

Our day started with Bronya's early wake-up shouts and it did not end until after dark (sometimes even until late in the evening if there were still trucks to be unloaded), interrupted only by a short lunch-break of watery soup with one small potato and a few pieces of turnip in it. Upon our return in the evening we received another thin soup, a bit of dark bread and sometimes a bit of sausage or a spoonful of cottage cheese. Our day ended with Bronya bellowing, '*Auf de* [sic] *Betten. Alles gait schlufen!*' [sic] (On the beds, all go to sleep!).

The camp kitchen had no salt left by the end of February. We knew that this would weaken us even further. One day I was given the chore to sprinkle rock salt on to the large weighing platform to clear the ice. I stuffed my coat pockets full of the pink salt and I managed to smuggle it into the dormitory. We reasoned that if animals ate this, why not sprinkle it into our watery soup? We distributed it among ourselves, sewing pockets from small linen scraps which Hanka and Hilde had 'organized' from the factory, to store the salt in. When none of us felt worse for eating it, we added it daily to our watery soup during the rest of our stay in Merzdorf.

There were certain tensions between the Czech and the Polish prisoners. I was part of the Czech contingent – there were few German Jews in this camp. The Polish kitchen personnel gave thin, watery soup to us and thick soup from the bottom of the kettle to their compatriots. That system existed unchallenged until the very end.

We 'organized' and ate a lot of flax seed, and since we worked outside the factory limits we had more opportunity to find frozen, half-decayed beets and potato peelings in the compost heap. We stuffed our pockets full of these edible treasures, sometimes we hid them under our dresses and coats and brought them into the shower, where we washed them carefully before greedily devouring them. We frequently ate plants and grass. I found a patch of horseradish roots which we dug up and smuggled back into our dormitory.

The Hungarian prisoners were always 'cooking'. They talked or rather dreamed out loud about food. They fantasized, describing recipes and apparently savouring the most wonderful culinary creations while they were lying on their bunks with their stomachs empty. We had constant confrontations with them, they were afraid of fresh air and did not want us to open the windows. Some of us literally had to fight with them to divert their attention long enough so that the rest of us could open some of the windows. A few minutes of air was better than none at all. Buschi used to say: 'Their motto is: better stink to death than freeze to death!' (*Besser erstinken als erfrieren*).

The cold and the ever-present lice were our worst enemies. We wore thin dresses and thin coats – no socks or underwear. Just thin kerchiefs around our shaven heads and aprons. January, February and even March were very cold months in the Silesian mountain region. A couple of our girls who worked in the factory 'organized' raw flax material for us. We made all kinds of body-warmers out of this, such as flax head-warmers which we wore under our kerchiefs. There were also flax chest-warmers, inserts for our wooden clogs and many other marvellous inventions. I am sure that we would not have been able to survive the bitterly cold winter without them.

Our girls who worked on the looms 'organized' enough scraps of linen material to make other useful items. Hilde and Hannah were endowed with ample breasts and their creation of a brassière was uniformly admired.

My great fear always was that I would break my glasses, which would render me more or less useless for work since I have always been very near-sighted. I still consider it a miracle that my one and only pair of glasses survived with me. I never dared to take them off my nose in Auschwitz and I found a safe night-time place for them on the bunk in Merzdorf.

Some of the German foremen were really brutal: they hit and abused the women and drove them to work harder and harder until they either collapsed or were close to doing so. Our so-called '*Meister*' was a short emaciated-looking man of about 50. He had a squirrel-like face with small unsteady eyes. He was missing several teeth and those he had left were brown and ugly-looking. His mouth was thin, his upper lip covered with a moustache and his short straw-coloured hair was partially greying around his temples.

Herr Meister often displayed his evil temper when any calamity occurred. We tried to load the wagons so that they would not turn over, but some disasters were inevitable. Sometimes the roads were muddy or slippery and it was difficult for us to control these huge vehicles. Zdena and I usually ended up taking the place of horses (*Deichselführer*) pulling and steering the handle in front of the wagon, and as I mentioned before, many additional hands would be pushing from the rear. We were just very lucky that we escaped injury when major mishaps occurred.

Sundays were the worst days for us. The commandant (*Frau Kommandantin*) usually had the most unpleasant surprises in store for us. We often wondered whether she spent all week plotting how to torture us on Sundays. Our 'day of rest' was spent in the courtyard in bitter winter weather with mass activities such as everyone having to have their hair shaved off. We would have to sweep the enormous courtyard, even though it did not need sweeping. The whole camp had to assemble in the yard, regardless of temperature or weather conditions, and stand at attention for hours on end. The prisoners were counted by the Nazi guards, sometimes over and over again. These were roll-calls without prisoner participation and we were not allowed to move.

Frau Kommandantin Erna Rinke, her fat face flushed and her huge body almost bursting out of its tight uniform, would shower us with verbal abuse. Her powerful, vulgar beer-barrel voice boomed through the courtyard: 'Take your paws out of your pockets' (*Pfoten von den Taschen*); 'Bones down!' (*Knochen herunter*); 'Otherwise I kick you in the ass!' (*Sonst trete ich Dich in den Arsch*); 'You dirty bitches' (*Ihr Sauweiber*); 'If you don't stand still, you can look at the food in the kettle!' (*wenn Ihr nicht still steht könnt Ihr Euch das Fressen im Pot ansehen!*) were just a few samples of her daily, especially Sunday, outbursts. We were ordered to do all kinds of dirty work for the Nazi guards. Their resourcefulness was unlimited. We were sure that they spent their sleepless nights dreaming up torments for us. Our living quarters would be fumigated. Our dormitory and every bunk had to be scrubbed. Their 'day of rest' was truly hell for us.

One Sunday I did not feel well – I was sure that I was running a fever. We had to stand in the yard for hours on a cold, damp and dreary day. Buschi stood in front of me and Zdena stood behind me. Buschi and Zdena were much taller than I so that they could shield me from the eyes of the guards. They both supported me as best as they could to prevent me from collapsing. The following day was Monday – a work day. Strangely enough I felt completely well again, and I put in my usual 10–12 hours of hard transport work. Except for this one brief episode, I never suffered from a cold or illness of any kind to the day of my liberation.

We experienced a number of air raid warnings during which time we were confined to our building as the guards locked all doors and windows. We were trapped. Had the factory suffered a direct hit we would have all perished.

Those of us in the transport group worked outside and seemed to stay much healthier than the girls who had to work in the factory. During our march to our work-site we would look at the beautiful Riesengebirge, those lovely, majestic snow-capped mountains of the Sudeten chain. How we longed to just run to them, climb them, escape to them.

We often met the war prisoners who were working for the factory. They would tell us the most recent political news. Unfortunately, they were much too optimistic. Maurice, who was a French prisoner of war, promised to take me into the mountains – a promise which on our liberation he kept.

In January and February 1945 we were threatened with total evacuation of the factory. We worried constantly about this, knowing that preparations had been made for it a number of times. It would have meant forced marches on the road in freezing temperatures, which many would not survive. We worried also that we would be transported to another concentration camp. Some of our fellow prisoners were so convinced that we would be evacuated that they attempted to escape, but unfortunately they had not planned it well. They were caught and the whole camp was punished. We were not given any food for 24 hours. Our hair had grown a little since Auschwitz, but now everybody was going to have a 10 cm strip shaved off the scalp from the forehead to the neckline. After one or two cuts the machine broke. Our joy was short-lived, however, as they found plenty of scissors to do the job.

The following Sunday they cut a 15 cm-wide and 25 cm-long strip out of our dress or coat, and then stitched a long strip of red cloth into the gap. On the Sunday that followed they painted a cross with white oil paint on the red stripe.

When we went to work early the next morning we saw innumerable caravans of people being evacuated towards the west. Foreign workers, prisoners from other camps – there were numerous labour, prisoner of war camps and a major concentration camp (Gross-Rosen) in this part of Silesia – some Germans with their small wooden carts, others with large horse-drawn wagons housing their whole family, children and grandparents and all their belongings. They had left their houses and farms because they were afraid of the

Russian troops which were approaching faster and faster. These country roads were full of German refugees. This was in the bitter cold weather of February and March in the mountain region of Silesia. The people were suffering terribly: they looked frozen, sick and frightened, but we had no sympathy for them: they were Germans. They had condoned what had been done to us and our families. We felt that they were getting what they deserved. The caravans scared us just the same because we realized that we would not survive should the SS force us on the road in an evacuation march. We reckoned they would probably shoot us on the way because they did not want to leave any evidence of their barbarous treatment, criminal acts and murders for the world to witness. As we learned later, they were quite successful in concealing their deeds.

By February and March 1945 it was evident to the Germans that the war was lost. They tried desperately to erase all marks of their misdeeds: their goal was to empty the camps and force the prisoners – the weak walking skeletons – into 'death marches', where they would either freeze or starve to death, or be shot because they could not keep up, or simply collapse.

One morning in February while walking to our work-site to unload a freight train we encountered a very long column of war prisoners who were on an evacuation march from a more easterly camp. As the column approached we recognized them as English prisoners of war. Our guard was busy flirting with their guard, so I used the opportunity to make myself busy close to them. (To us, every prisoner or foreigner was like a brother!)

Suddenly I heard somebody say in English, 'Be strong, poor sisters, war will be finished very soon. Be silent! *Amcho Yisroel* [of the people of Israel].' The soldier clearly wanted to convey to me that he was Jewish. I was so happy but I did not look at him and I remained silent as he asked. Had the Germans known that he was Jewish they would have shot him. Just hearing his encouraging words, however, gave me so much strength.

The Russians were getting closer in February 1945, but they

did not reach us for a very long time. Every week seemed like an eternity. Our camp was gradually running out of food, our rations were getting smaller and smaller, but they expected us to work more and more. One day some of our fellow prisoners told a foreman that we were getting so little food that we just could not keep up with the pace of the work. He mentioned this to the factory director who in turn complained to the SS commander at the concentration camp Gross-Rosen, who had ultimate charge of our camp, and who also was the superior of our commandant, Erna Rinke. The factory director had apparently accused our commandant of diverting our food to enrich herself on the black market.

We were still hoping to receive more food, when several days later we were ordered to leave our work and assemble in the factory yard. There we faced five tall brutal-looking SS officers of the Auschwitz type, dressed in their immaculate uniforms, high leather boots and leather gloves. Suddenly one of them started to scream at us: 'You lousy Jewish bitches [*Ihr Judensauweiber*], if you think you can commit sabotage here you are mistaken. I warn you, if you mention one more word about food, tomorrow you'll be hanging here from these trees!' (*Wenn Ihr Judenweiber glaubt, Ihr könnt hier Sabotage treiben, dann irrt Ihr Euch, noch ein Wort vom Fressen und Ihr hängt hier alle von den Bäumen!*). He was very persuasive. We did not complain about food anymore; we just slowly starved.

After cleaning the platform of the industrial scale, I would step on it and see my weight dwindle day by day. One evening it was already dark and we were on our way back from work when I found a frozen piece of meat in the road; we had no idea what kind of animal it came from. I picked it up and hid it under my dress and coat. In the shower we took turns washing it under hot water: we managed to thaw it out and then devoured it raw. We never knew what it was that we ate, but none of us became sick.

Hannah suffered under a vicious foreman with a terrible temper. She worked in the spinnery where spindles twisted the yarn into thread. There was often breakage of the yarn which had to be knotted very fast or the whole production line of 80 spindles had to be stopped. One day, poor Hannah found herself exactly in that predicament, as hard as she tried, she could not knot the many breaks fast enough. The foreman became so enraged that he came close to killing her with a heavy wrench.

Both Hannah and Buschi had to spend some time in the sick-bay as they were both very ill. Buschi came down with an infection, which I believe was scarlet fever, while Hannah had acute abdominal pain. I was lucky – I didn't even get a cold!

We had two sisters in our transport section: Leah and Vera Nettle from Prague. Leah was heavily pregnant. She was able to conceal her pregnancy until the ninth month but we were very worried about her and did as much as we could to help her sister to protect her. Leah managed to keep on working – it was very difficult for her, but it was her only chance of staying alive. During February and March she would occasionally rest in an open shed by the tracks where we were unloading the freight trucks. Her sister Vera would cover her with straw to hide her from view of the foreman and the Nazi guard. Our group leader Bronka must have been aware of the situation, but she pretended not to see it. The baby was born in Merzdorf shortly before our liberation.*

From the beginning of April we started to hear powerful explosions almost on a daily basis. Our work remained the same: long hours of heavy pulling and lifting. The guards got meaner and crueller. Our Belgian and French war prisoner friends kept encouraging us, and indeed gave us great hope, but we were getting weaker and we could not envisage an end to our ordeal.

On 24 April 1945 my friends celebrated my birthday in the evening after work. Buschi had found a penknife in the garbage dump. She gave it to me with the following poem written in pencil on a piece of toilet paper:

---

*Lily Sobotka, who was a midwife assistant in Theresienstadt, used her skills to deliver little Thomas in Merzdorf. She recalls in a recent kibbutz newsletter that in March 1945 she had only scissors and rags to deliver the baby. Leah Nettle had to report back to her 12-hour shift almost immediately after giving birth, to give herself and little Thomas a chance to live.

I learned only several months ago that Leah and Vera Nettle live in Australia. Leah's son Thomas has a PhD in chemistry.

Ein eigener Herd, ein Sprichwort heisst,
Ist Goldes wert, wie du ja weisst.
Kann ich den eigenen Herd nicht geben
Nimm ich Ersatz, wie oft im Leben.
Ist dieses Messer auch nicht neu
Ich dir's zu geben doch nicht scheu.
Denn ich habe stets danach gestrebt
Wer gibt was er hat
Ist wert dass er lebt.

(One's own hearth, the saying goes,
Is worth its weight in gold, as you know
If I cannot give your own hearth to you
I shall substitute, as so often in life.
Even though this knife is not new,
I won't hesitate to give it to you.
It has always been my thought
He who gives what he has
deserves to live.)

I was grateful that all six of us were together again. Hannah and Buschi had recovered, despite the fact that there were no medical facilities and practically no medicines available and that the 'doctor' of the sick-bay was a dentist by profession.

The girls had made small paper-thin sandwiches, decorated with slices of potato. Everyone had saved a potato from the daily soup. They gave me handkerchiefs which they had sewn from discarded linen scraps. I was so moved, I cried. I felt that I had been so lucky that pure chance had thrown me together with such wonderful selfless human beings who kept their dignity in spite of the adversity, ugliness and greed. I also remembered my birthday in Theresienstadt the year before, when my brother had given me several little presents. He had written on each one of them, 'To my dear sister.'

After returning from work one evening in April, I was walking up the stairs in our building when a Nazi guard coming down from the kitchen met me on the staircase. I immediately and respectfully stepped aside to make room for her, as was expected of any prisoner. She was carrying a large porcelain dish loaded with food. She was a big woman with a face that reminded me of a fat pig. Suddenly she pushed her dish toward me and said: *'Friss'* (Eat!). What a feast we had: mashed potatoes and sauerkraut! I just could not believe my luck. That was the first time that a Nazi guard had given me something to eat. While we were enjoying the food we wondered out loud whether this could indeed be a good omen.

I think it was the first day of May when we were working at the railway station, and we could not believe our eyes as we saw a notice posted on one of the columns – 'HITLER IS DEAD'. First we did not dare believe it, then our spirits began to soar, but euphoria was quickly replaced by worries. What would the SS do to us now?

On 7 May they still wanted to evacuate us. The French and Belgians had emphasized over and over: 'Refuse to be herded into the road, the Russians are only 20 kilometres outside of Merzdorf!' We knew that this was good advice, but how could we implement it? How could we refuse to obey orders to assemble for a death march if the command was enforced with loaded machine guns?

In the evening of 7 May the SS locked all the windows and doors. Many of the Hungarian women were convinced that we would be gassed right there in the building. During the night we heard a lot of commotion in the factory yard, with the sound of vehicles arriving and leaving. The SS and the women guards were yelling and hurrying around. It sounded to us that they were dragging heavy loads along the corridors. Suitcases were being loaded into big trucks which were parked in the yard. Everybody was whispering: 'They are leaving and we are locked in!' We feared that we would be trapped in the building if the factory were bombed or set on fire.

15 · *Liberation*

In the early morning of 8 May 1945, the heavy door of our quarters was unlocked and opened by a German soldier. He was all by himself. Struggling with his words, he began, 'Ladies … ' (*Meine Damen*). We looked at each other – was he talking to us? We were only used to being addressed as 'dirty bitches' (*Sauweiber*). He continued, 'You are free, your guards have departed' (*Sie sind frei, Ihre Bewachung ist abgereist*). And he left.

We just did not grasp it. We were still too scared to feel happy. We did not dare leave the camp until Maurice and the other war prisoners pulled us out of there and took us to the mountains, and ran with us through the beautiful valley. We were free – it slowly sank in. One minute we felt like small children allowed to walk on their own, the next like wild animals who had broken out of their cages.

We were so terribly starved, we could only think of food. The six of us went from one farmhouse to the other. We no longer had any fear of Germans who had decided to stay. They were afraid of us now. In one farmhouse we were invited to sit at a huge table. They were serving steaming potatoes cooked in their skins. There were two huge earthenware bowls in the middle of the table: one contained the potatoes, the other was filled with cottage cheese. We were invited to help ourselves. We ate like pigs, mostly with our hands. We could not shovel it down fast enough, potatoes, skins and all. The farmers and their helpers stopped eating, they just watched us in amazement, as you might watch animals.

We went to a store, where we ate marmalade by the shovelful. We ate and drank so much that our starved bodies could not cope. We felt sick and could not digest the milk and the fats. We were lucky that we vomited it all up. In fact we got rid of it from both ends in a beautiful meadow in Merzdorf.

About 1 p.m. the first Russian scout arrived on a bicycle. The Czech girls were able to communicate with this soldier. A short time later a Russian motorized troop appeared. They first visited the girls in the sick-bay, then they gave us cigarettes and tried to give us anything we asked for. The grocer who had provided our camp (and who had black-marketed many of our food supplies) was ordered to supply us with anything we desired, *and* to package it for us! We plundered his store with the enthusiastic help of the Russians.

Hannah, Hanka, Zdena, Hilde, Buschi and I were as inseparable after liberation as we had been during our imprisonment. We paid scant attention to our fellow prisoners who had slept close to us and worked with us but who had never reached out to us – the last prisoners to arrive at the factory.

We were still going around in rags. We went from one deserted German or SS villa to another, and we took anything we could get our hands on with little regard to whether it would fit: clothing and shoes, and most importantly underwear, which we had not seen (never mind worn) for eight months.

Our first and foremost interest was still food, food and more food. We did not see our foremen (*Meisters*) any more. The SS had fled with the women guards. I could not get my desired revenge of shaving off *Frau Kommandantin* Erna Rinke's hair. We could not even give the sly, treacherous Bronya a haircut or a beating – she had bolted from the camp as soon as the doors were opened.

We could not sleep in the camp anymore. Everything was a total mess. All the toilets were stopped up. Like us, our fellow prisoners had also eaten too much and could not digest the sudden intake of rich foods. Many got very sick, throwing up in and over their beds. We six decided it was time to leave the camp.

The following morning, 9 May, we discovered the deserted

villa of an SS doctor at the edge of the village. The villa had already been plundered. In the attic we found glasses of preserved onions and pickles which we enjoyed immensely. By now we had accumulated more loot than we knew how to transport. The great find of a baby carriage in the cellar solved our problem. Then, in the afternoon, Buschi and I met a Russian officer who spoke English. He urged us to leave Merzdorf and return to the countries we came from as soon as possible, because he was convinced that the borders, now still open, could soon be closed.

After some deliberation Buschi and I decided to stay with our Czech friends and head towards Prague. We reasoned that from a large city with an extensive transportation centre like Prague, there would be a better chance for us to eventually reach our destinations: Lippborg and Amsterdam.

We spent the night in the doctor's villa. We thoroughly searched every nook and cranny in the house, opened every drawer and every closet, and were delighted when we found underwear, dresses and various other kinds of clothing. We promptly tried it all on under the watchful eyes of the family pictures still hanging on the walls. We used the luxurious bathing facilities for a major cleansing job, including a delousing inspection of each other.

Hanka was immediately drawn to the piano. I admired her ability to play an instrument so beautifully. (I had always wished that I could do so myself.) I was overwhelmed by it all. We were overcome with emotion: we laughed and cried and we worried about our families. Until recently we had been struggling simply to survive; now we could think beyond mere survival, and all those nagging fears were resurfacing. I knew that I would never see my father and brother again. I wondered whether my mother had survived the war. Was she still in Vienna? Who would I find in Lippborg – the small village not too far from the Dutch–German border where my Aunt Minchen lived, the place my parents had designated for our reunion?

We set the table carefully with the SS doctor's china and silverware, and we made a great effort to eat in a more civilized manner, using knives and forks instead of our fingers. We gave thanks for our deliverance from Hell. That evening our feelings flowed freely, stirring and touching each one of us. That night we slept in real beds – we even had to get used to that again, and some of us woke up on the floor.

Next morning, 10 May, we had just finished breakfast when our solitary Russian *Jewish* soldier on his bike paid us a surprise visit. Buschi and I were grateful that our Czech friends were able somehow to communicate with him. He told us that he had to move on, but before doing so he ordered some fleeing Germans in their wagons to hand over their bikes to us. He called them '*machinas*'. He tried each one out, discarded those he found wanting into the ditch until he had convinced himself that he had found six sturdy '*machinas*' which would get us home. Indeed, the two '*machinas*' which he gave to Buschi and me eventually brought us back to the country where I was born, but it would never be home again.

There were no trains running anywhere. On 10 May we left Merzdorf with our bicycles but not before receiving a stern warning from our soldier friend: 'Do not accept lifts from anyone, including Russian soldiers.' It never occurred to us then how vulnerable we were.

Directly after my liberation I had the urge to write about my experiences. I made some rough notes on pieces of paper while we were still on the road. Later I copied them into a diary which my aunt gave me after we arrived at her house in western Germany. I still have that diary and it has been invaluable in telling my story.

16 · Journey to Lippborg

Our road to Prague was to lead us through parts of the Sudetenland, that large border region between Bohemia, Moravia and Germany where many Germans had lived for generations. Czech territory after World War I, the region was annexed by Hitler in 1938. The deep-seated Czech–German ethnic animosities in the Sudetenland are centuries old, and most Germans fled from their homes in the spring of 1945. The first place we reached on our bicycles was Landeshut (Kamienno Gora), a small town near the Czech–German border and the River Elbe. Buschi and I had more endurance at bicycling than our friends who became exhausted very quickly, so that we had to push our bikes a good part of the way.

The nameplate on an abandoned house we came to told us that the Knappes had lived there. We spent the night of 10 May in that place which had already been plundered thoroughly. We cooked and ate dinner there. We repeatedly expressed thanks for our new-found freedom, but worries and fears about our families, especially the men, took the edge off our spirits.

We moved on in the morning of 11 May, when we came upon a deserted farmhouse. We hid our bikes in the bushes before cautiously entering. The doors were wide open, and frightened calves were running through the house. We witnessed an incredible scene. Soldiers had probably spent the night there. They had slaughtered the chickens in the bedroom. They had broken practically every piece of furniture in the house. They had cut open the feather bedding and torn the sheets. Every glass jar of preserved food had been opened and a lot of it had been eaten. They had boiled countless chickens in a huge kettle which was normally used to boil wash in. Chicken feathers were covering everything.

Cooked potatoes were lying on the stove, which was still warm. We had a most generous breakfast from the leftovers of the previous looters, and pushed on to Liebau (Lubawka).

At Liebau we spotted a simple cottage, and asked the old woman who answered the door for shelter. She invited us to spend the night with her. She lived alone and was terrified of the Russians. In the evening, while we were all stark naked, busily washing ourselves, the door creaked open and a Russian soldier entered the hut. We tried to grab anything to cover ourselves, except for Buschi who was looking at the soldier like Eve with shorn hair, transfixed, unable to move. The Russian soldier either found the choice too plentiful or not to his taste. He simply turned around and closed the door behind him. We exhaled deeply in a chorus of relief and resumed washing ourselves.

The small towns and villages through which we passed showed hardly any signs of wartime destruction, they just seemed empty, dismally quiet: there were no people, no cars or trucks or horse-drawn wagons on these country roads. The people who had not fled were hiding in their houses. I do not recall seeing any children anywhere. Czech partisans and Germans were still fighting; occasionally we heard shooting in the distance while we were on the road.

On 12 May, we hiked to a village called Binsdorf. During the day we always looked for food. We had become experts at 'organizing' to satisfy our stomachs. We did not hesitate to knock on the doors of private houses or stores and ask for whatever we wanted, nor did we have any scruples about entering deserted farms, stores and homes to help ourselves to whatever we needed.

On 13 May we came to another small place called Goldenoels. We were lucky to knock on the door of the Pilzes, a very nice Czech family who truly welcomed us. They put us up for the night and treated us to a good meal. While some people like the Pilz family were genuinely interested and sympathetic and asked many questions, many Germans who gave us shelter and food were defensive, and did so only out of fear. They really did not want to find out what had happened to us. They pre-empted any dialogue with: 'We were not Nazis, and we did not know, and what could we have done? And now we have to suffer!'

At the Pilzes we met Edmont, a Polish Jew, and like us a survivor of a concentration camp. He helped us bake *Palatschinken* (Czech omelettes), and the Pilzes gave us home-made jam to fill them with. We had a feast, but the horrible stories of his experiences in the camp further dimmed any hope of finding our menfolk alive.

We parted the next morning: Edmont travelled east to search for his family, and we continued in the direction of Trautenau (Trutnov, Czechoslovakia). We were worried because Czech partisans were still about who had made it their mission to search out any Germans and Nazis who had not fled. Ironicaly that put us in danger because we could not speak Czech, and in partisan eyes anyone speaking German was suspect. So Buschi and I felt safe in the company of our Czech friends, and we let them do the talking for us.

On 14 May we arrived in Trautenau. At this point Hannah fell ill and could not go on. She was near collapse and had severe chest pains. We had to take her to the hospital where we were told that she had suffered a heart attack and needed prolonged medical care. She encouraged us to go on without her. It was a terrible decision for us to make, but in the end we all agreed that we had no choice. Very reluctantly and sadly we left her at the Trautenau hospital.

The remaining five of us spent the night in Farmer Kindler's hayloft in the outskirts of the town. The next morning we were allowed to bathe at the Beckers. We were so appreciative – a bath was a rare luxury. We met German and Dutch (non-Jewish) former concentration camp prisoners, who urged us not to head for Prague because foreigners and former concentration camp inmates were being rounded up and put into transit camps. And so after much discussion, we decided that Buschi and I should leave our Czech friends and try to head for Lippborg.

It was traumatic for each of us to say goodbye after having been so close and so committed a group of friends. We might never see each other again.* The bond that held us together

*Neither Buschi, Hannah, Zdenka nor I ever saw or heard from Anka Konigova or Hilde Sonnenberg again.

was being broken. The support we had given to each other would not be there anymore. Now we had to fend for ourselves.

Buschi and I had only bicycled a few hours when we experienced our first flat tyre. We turned the bicycle upside down, resting it on the saddle and handle bars and were trying to work out how to take the tyre off, when as luck would have it, 'George', a former Belgian prisoner of war, passed us on his bike. He offered his help and expertly fixed the tyre. He wished us well, and Buschi and I continued our journey.

Many Germans were consumed by fear of the advancing Russian army. Stories of rape and retribution made them abandon their homes and apartments and flee to the West, leaving all their belongings behind. Buschi and I cautiously entered these deserted places; we had no hesitation about helping ourselves to whatever was edible or useful. At times our bikes were so overloaded that we had to forgo some of the booty. Somewhere in one apartment we picked up writing paper, pens and pencils. I had the urge to write down what had happened to me. I think I wrote my first notes about my experiences in the camps at the side of a road where we had stopped to rest, and then made daily entries during the many weeks of bicycling to Lippborg.

The roads were almost completely deserted. We were told that Czech partisans were still fighting Germans all through the border areas, and received many warnings to stay off the main highways. The weather had been perfect ever since our liberation. The fields were lush. The trees were leafy and wild flowers bloomed in abundance. At midday it sometimes became too hot, especially when we had to pedal our bikes up mountainous roads. Unfortunately there were more mountains in the Sudeten region than we had bargained for.

After pushing our bikes up a steep hilly road we rested at the edge of a wooded area. There we saw a dead German soldier. Timidly we searched his pockets and found a military map of Germany. Of course it had a swastika printed on it, but never mind that, the map was a life-saver! Being very detailed, it allowed us to check the directions people gave us in the villages, and to find alternate routes when desirable or necessary. Buschi was much better at reading the map than I was. We put together some sort of a travel plan, realizing full well that given the uncertain conditions there probably would have to be many changes. The map shocked us into the realization that we had a very long, arduous trip ahead of us.

We reached a level road and were enjoying the effortless cycling when we were overtaken by a column of Russian soldiers on horseback. Their Asian features told us that they were probably Tartars. Suddenly one of the soldiers jumped off his horse and pulled on my bicycle carrier forcing me to stop and jump off my bike. Some of his comrades were also approaching fast with their horses. They made clicking sounds with their tongues and shouted to us in Russian. Their intentions could not have been clearer. We were paralysed with fear. This moustached, wild-looking soldier who had stopped my bike was coming closer to me, and just as he was starting to touch me, an officer approached on his horse. Buschi pulled her kerchief off and called out to me to do the same, exposing our shorn scalps. She tried to convey to him that 'we are Dutch, Holland', and that we had been prisoners in a German concentration camp.

The officer, still on his horse, gave some commands which we did not understand, and then used his horse-whip full force on my prospective rapist, who scrambled back on his horse. The officer indicated to us with gestures to continue our travel. Our panic gradually dissipated. Fortunately, we never experienced an incident like that again during our whole journey. (We never forgot it either!)

We reached the town of Hohenelbe (Vrchlabi). There, in a small local restaurant, we enjoyed the best soup we had ever eaten, but then we took a wrong turning and ended up in Hennersdorf (Dolni Branna), somewhat out of our way. Still we felt lucky, because there an old lady welcomed us into her house and generously supplied us with food and lodging for the night.

On 16 May, we backtracked to Hohenelbe. Next we passed through Tannenwald (Tanvald), another little town. There was no way of avoiding the steep narrow Laissor Pass. Hot and sweaty, we pushed our bicycles up the pass. We were stopped five times by armed partisans who were still searching for Nazis and who obviously did not trust us. Though my sentiments were with them I was terrified, although I tried not to show it.

Until Trautenau all of us had pretended to be Czech, but after our separation from our Czech friends this was no longer possible because we did not speak the language. As I mentioned earlier, it was dangerous to be German, or even to be heard speaking German. So now both of us were Dutch, only I was not allowed to utter a word since I did not speak Dutch either. Most Czechs speak and understand German. Dutch and German, of course, have some similarity, and Buschi managed to communicate with the partisans. Using gestures and her Dutch, she explained to them that I was still in shock and that I had lost my ability to speak. We had no identification whatsoever. The Czechs warned us that concentration camp guards were still abroad, that female guards had resorted to shaving their hair and were pretending to be former camp inmates. Their warning was very stern: 'Don't trust anybody on the road!'

We spent that night with a Czech family and pretended not to understand a word of German. We were allowed to cook for ourselves. We had soup, mashed potatoes, eggs and coffee. We slept well, even though we had to share a narrow sofa.

On 17 May we were stopped twice in Morgenstern. Our shaven heads were our only affidavit. The partisans were looking for our tattoos, which we could not produce, and since we did not speak Czech our explanations were suspect. Feeling more and more uncomfortable, we bicycled to the limit of our endurance just to get out of the Sudeten area.

We had obtained some scraps of white, blue and red material. At the edge of a meadow we sewed our Dutch flags (*orange, blanche, bleu* – red, white and blue are the colours of the Dutch flag) and wore them on our outer clothing.

After one of those frustrating encounters with partisans, I was again relegated to play the psychologically damaged, crazy girl, when I rebelled. I accused Buschi of being too bossy and literally treating me like an idiot. I declared that I was going off on my own, come what may. I had had enough! I rode off and she followed me, and of course we made up with big hugs and declarations of (if not eternal) enduring love during our earthly stay. I think it was the only major row we ever had.

We desperately needed identification papers. After many unsuccessful attempts Buschi finally succeeded in persuading the officer in charge at a Russian military post to issue us a rather unofficial-looking travel pass, written in Russian on a small scrappy piece of paper, but bearing an official-looking stamp. We had no idea what it said, but it did have our names on it. It worked like magic when we told people in the villages that this was a Russian order to supply us with food and shelter.

We passed through Gablonz (Jablonec) and shortly before Reichenberg we picnicked in the woods. In Reichenberg we were able to catch a freight train to Bodenbach. We arrived there about seven o'clock in the evening and we were allowed to sleep on the floor in the community building. Our Merzdorf camp blankets, with our concentration camp numbers still stitched on them, were useful that night. We dragged them around with us through Germany and beyond. (It has been more than 50 years since my liberation from Merzdorf, but I still have my blanket!)

We had hardly left Bodenbach at 8 a.m. on 18 May, when we had a flat tyre. We returned to Bodenbach to have it fixed but it took until 3 p.m. before we were back on the road again. While waiting to have the bike repaired, we met a man, about 30 years old, whom we dubbed '*Genosse* X' (Comrade X). He bragged that he was an influencial communist functionary with important connections. He suggested that we travel with him to Dresden. It was scary for two women to travel alone on deserted roads, so we gladly accepted.

We never entered the centre of Dresden; when passing it we saw a city almost totally destroyed. Rubble was strewn everywhere. Many façades were still standing while the rest of the buildings were pulverized. This city of ruins had an eerie, almost ghost-like quality. Damaged utility and gas lines posed a real danger. The roads were pock-marked with craters and blocked to cars and pedestrians, street lights were bent like straws. We looked at this destruction and felt no pity for the loss of a great city or indeed for the plight of its inhabitants.

We were worried about the difficulties we would encounter at the demarcation line between the Russian and American forces. We were told that it was virtually impossible to get across, since the border was officially closed at the town of Rochlitz at the River Mulde. The flat tyre had cost us a lot of time, and even though we did not leave until three o'clock in the afternoon, we pedalled 70 kilometres on that day, constantly trying to keep up with our new travel companion. It was a particularly strenuous trip for us.

We spent the night near Dresden in Dresden-Lochwitz in a deserted house. We each had a bed to ourselves. We had brought some food with us, and we drank some fruit wine which we found in the laundry room in the cellar of the house. We collapsed into our beds. The next morning 'Comrade X' woke us very early and we were back on our bikes by 6.30 a.m. We met a couple of young fellows on the road: one from Bremen, the other from Vienna. Their past history was not clear to us. They became chummy with 'Comrade X' and before we realized it, all three of them had disappeared with my precious, recently 'organized' jacket.

We rode our bikes another 50 kilometres past Freyburg. When we arrived in the village of Möbendorf we were totally worn out. We rang the bell of one of the first houses we came upon and were relieved that the Freund family allowed us to spend the night with them.

The next day, 20 May was a holiday called Pfingsten (Whitsuntide). We slept until 10.30 in the morning and then headed for Rochlitz on the River Mulde. On our way there we met two American former prisoners of war. They invited us to have a beer with them. I think Buschi actually enjoyed it. I thought it tasted awful, but I drank it anyway without batting an eyelid. After all, I was trying to impress two handsome American soldiers: I was drinking beer with them; I was speaking English with them. It was all terribly exciting and of course Buschi and I thought that they were 'very nice guys' (*schrecklich nette Kerle*)!

Buschi and I spent the night in the hayloft of Farmer Steudten. Very early in the morning of 21 May we arrived in Rochlitz on the River Mulde – the demarcation line! This line ran through the middle of the river, with Russian soldiers posted at the bridge on the east side of the river and American soldiers on the west side. It was forbidden to cross over. First we tried to cross at 6 a.m.: we showed our Russian 'pass' and the Russian soldier let us through, but when we came to the middle of the bridge the American soldier on guard duty refused to let us go on. We talked to him repeatedly and kept trying to cross. Finally, Buschi managed to have some personal exchange with him. His buddy was watching us from his post. Little by little we conveyed to him who we were, where we came from and where we wanted to go. 'I am also Jewish, but orders are orders', he said. 'We have strict orders and no exceptions are allowed!' Then he added: 'You might try to cross at exactly 8.15 a.m., that's when we change guards but now you *have* to go back!'

At exactly 8.15 a.m. we crossed the bridge, our two soldiers were busy with their telephones, shouting to each other about not getting any connection. When we reached them, they were both crouching around the field telephone, facing away from us, pretending not to see us, and without turning their heads toward us, they shouted at us: 'Get out of here as fast as you can!' We pedalled as if the devil himself was pursuing us, and reached the other side – the American zone!

Riding through the small village of Geithain we were able to obtain bread at the local bakery with our Russian 'pass'. The baker's wife at first insisted that she could not give us anything, but when Buschi demanded bread, telling her it was a Russian order to supply us with food, the woman quickly changed her mind. In fact the pass proved to be a valuable multipurpose document in both the American- and English-occupied zones of Germany.

After our liberation we had travelled through the German–Czech border areas until shortly before we reached Dresden. Somehow we felt fairly free and unencumbered travelling through this section of the country from which most Germans had fled; however, once we reached the

American-occupied zone of Germany we both felt quite uncomfortable. It was a peculiar sensation: one of not feeling welcome, even though nobody told us so. I almost felt as if I was trespassing on foreign hostile soil – these people had been my foes, my persecutors, the killers of my father and my brother. It was a feeling that never left me during the two post-war years I spent in Germany.

Our journey, destination Lippborg, led us (not always by the most direct route) through many, mostly small, places, some of them not even on our precious map. We were not too far into the American zone before we reached Borna, where Captain Rogins received us in his office. He was sitting at his desk with his feet resting upon it – he never changed that position the whole time he was conversing with us. We thought Captain Rogins' manners rather strange but perhaps totally acceptable in America. He sent us to the villa of the former magistrate, which he had confiscated to provide shelter for some Dutch (non-Jewish) displaced persons who had been deported into forced labour by the Nazis. He was in the process of arranging a transport for them to get them home.

I had to be deaf and dumb again. For me to pretend to be Dutch among Dutch people and not to speak the language was horrible. Buschi made it clear to them that I was a little crazy (*meschugge*). Buschi met a very nice Dutch girl who had lived in Prague. She very much wanted us to join their transport 'home'. I felt so terribly uncomfortable among these people who tried to comfort me and felt sorry for me. They constantly talked to me in Dutch, I so strongly felt their pity that I started to feel depressed and helpless at the same time. I tried to persuade Buschi to take advantage of this opportunity to go back to Holland, but she would not leave me. She vowed to accompany me to Lippborg, and so we left her compatriots. (She had explained to them that I was dreadfully afraid of transports and camps, and I would suffer even more of a relapse if she forced me to join them.)

We were back on the road again, and we pushed on to Pulkau and Peres. Luckily we rang the right door bell, and found shelter with two beds and a good meal.

On 22 May we had breakfast at five o'clock in the morning

and rode on to Weissenfels and Wethau, where we spent the night with Frau Philippzig, a nice, but very peculiar old lady who shared her double bed with us. She gave us bread with lard and cake for the road. On 23 May we went on to Naumburg. We were constantly being stopped and asked for identification papers. 'Foreigners have to go into collection camps [*Auffangslager*]', we were told. The MPs (American Military Police) were not impressed with our Russian 'passes'.

We went to the US military government office, but they refused to supply us with a pass. We assured them that we would present ourselves at the next collection camp. So we pedalled on to Freyburg and Bibra.

In Bibra we stopped at a restaurant to ask for food. They gave us a wonderful meal with fresh asparagus. (We had not seen asparagus for years!) Flowers were blooming everywhere: in the window-boxes outside the restaurant; in the gardens of the small towns and villages; in the meadows; on bushes and trees. The sky was blue, the sun was shining and the world looked so beautiful. We had not seen this world for many years. Every morning as we pedalled through the countryside I was filled with awe.

On we went to Saubach, where the Wengels invited us to share a meal with them – our second full meal of the day. They also provided us with pillows and blankets, and we slept that night in their hayloft.

A difficult day for us was 24 May. On the way to Kölleda we were stopped four times. We had no papers, and we asked to see the American officer in charge there, a Lieutenant Brownfield. We begged him to give us a pass, but he was nasty and insolent, and threw us out.

We were getting more and more apprehensive: it seemed almost inevitable that we would end up in a camp again. We were being stopped at roadblocks and checkpoints, and soldiers would steer us to the nearest collection camp for foreigners and displaced persons. They relied on our promise that we would follow their instructions, which we had no intention of doing! The very idea of any camp, no matter under whose auspices, was unacceptable to us. In fact the idea filled us with panic.

We entered Straussfurt at 9.30 p.m., and we still managed

to obtain one bed and supper. The weather continued to be beautiful: sometimes a little too hot, but really ideal for 'tramps' like us. I don't believe we had a rainy day during our whole trip.

On 25 May we came to Bad Tennstedt, where we were treated to the worst cheese-cake imaginable, made from very ripe goat's milk. We met another Dutchman, and I had to be deaf and dumb again! Herr Albers, the mayor of Bad Tennstedt was very sympathetic. He gave us a pass which was valid in the ten-kilometre radius of the town; outside that, however, it was useless. We decided to sew Dutch flags and attach them to our bikes, hoping that the flags would gain us unrestricted passage.

On we went on to Grossgottern. Even though we were displaying our Dutch colours; we were stopped 20 times! It was not easy, but somehow we convinced each one of the military patrols to let us pass.

Buschi was a wonderful 'organizer'. I would watch our bikes while she would do the rounds from one store or door of an apartment or private home to another. She would ask in her polite cultured German for food, lodging or whatever else we were lacking at that moment. She usually explained that we had been imprisoned in a concentration camp and that we were on our way home to Holland. There, in Grossgottern, I can still see her crossing the road beaming, walking towards me, where I was waiting for her with our bikes, her whole bearing signifying triumph and accomplishment. I never had to ask her: 'Did they give you anything?' I could tell a mile away: she was either grinning, or downcast. Of course, she had done it again: what a cache of wonderful foods and goodies!

It was early evening when we rang the bell of a house in Flarchheim. A woman opened the door and curtly asked us what we wanted. Buschi asked her if she could put us up for the night, explaining that we were on our way home and that we had no place to stay. She grudgingly told us to enter when her husband appeared in the doorway. A surly man, he did not greet us, but rather gave us a suspicious look and then disappeared into another room. 'You can sleep there', she said with loathing and disdain, pointing to a sofa in an open vestibule. It was the first time that we felt uncomfortable with our hosts and we were glad to leave early the next morning.

On 26 May we arrived in Schwebda where we spent the night in a bakery. We were given a small room with one bed. We did not feel as uneasy with these people as we had felt the previous night with the family in Flarchheim, but a few things that were said convinced us that the baker and his family were (former?) Nazis. When I visited their outhouse early in the morning of 27 May, I found pieces of newspaper stuck on a nail to be used as toilet paper. As I was reading some of the newspaper pieces, I came across the heading: 'News from Eschwege'. I told Buschi that my grandmother came from this area, and I remembered that a brother of hers had been living in that town before I was deported. I had only met her brother Heinrich (they called him Henner) a few times when I was a child.

So we headed for Eschwege which was not very far and actually on our way. We had no trouble locating the Füllgrafs, and were warmly received by the old couple who could not do enough for us. We felt relaxed and comfortable with them – they treated us like family. In the afternoon we all went for a walk and picked flowers. This was our first day of actual rest and recreation since we left Merzdorf. They treated us to wonderful, home-cooked food, and we were especially grateful for the relaxing hot bath they provided. All four of us slept in their only bedroom, two to each bed. Even though we were dog-tired, we were kept awake by Heinrich's wife, who tried to cheer us up with dirty jokes. Most of them I did not even understand, but Buschi evidently did because she kept referring to my 'vulgar relative'! (When I later related this to my grandmother, she showed neither surprise nor shock. Her only comment was: 'She has obviously not changed. I am so grateful that they took good care of you and Buschi.')

We left the Füllgrafs and Eschwege in the afternoon of 28 May. We were warned to remove our Dutch flags because 'All foreigners are forced into camps now!' We heeded the warnings. We reached Frieda, where we had to cross the River Aue with our bikes. The bridge was badly damaged and crossing it, we felt like tightrope walkers.

In Langenhain-Vilmeden a very nice old lady put us up for

the night. Her cake was the best we had eaten in years, or maybe ever! On 29 May we left Langenhain-Vilmeden. It took us four hours to tackle the mountainous road and we were constantly on our guard to avoid checkpoints, and the most feared consequences – camps. At Rommerode we had to travel on a dangerously steep road, but by doing so we managed to circumvent the controls again.

We ran into all sorts of people on the road of different ethnic, cultural, religious and political backgrounds: prisoners of war, former inmates of concentration and labour camps; men, women and children, all displaced by the war. We listened to their stories: some we believed, whilst others were questionable. We wondered if any of the friendly travellers we met up with were actually former concentration camp guards. Generally there was a lot of camaraderie, sharing of information and helpfulness. This certainly served us well to avoid the roadblocks and checkpoints.

We continued on to Helsa. We found a beautiful room in Oberkaufungen. On 30 May we reached the outskirts of Kassel. All the bridges had been blown up and we had to cross the River Fulda by ferry. Kassel looked very much like Dresden, having suffered enormous destruction. We avoided as much of the city as we could.

We proceeded to Warburg. A German woman in her early thirties welcomed us into her home. Her living room and her bedroom were filled with pictures of her husband in German military uniform. Her husband had been fighting on the eastern front and she feared for him. She wanted to give us shelter, hoping that people would be similarly kind to him. As she put it: 'He could be knocking on someone's door just like you did.' I felt empathy with her: she seemed a decent person. She wanted to know about us and she wanted to listen, and she never used the clichés we heard from many of the German families with whom we stayed: 'I didn't know and what could I do?'

I felt deeply angry when they said, 'I didn't know.' How could they not have known when their own children sang the Hitler Youth songs which told the story? I was recently reminded of one such song which I heard so many times. This is one of its stanzas: 'When Jewish blood squirts from the knife' (*Wenn's Judenblut vom Messer spritzt*). We were assured by so many people that they had never been Nazis. These solemn declarations brought back to me memories of the huge Nazi rallies which I witnessed as a child and teenager. In my mind's eye I could see hundreds of thousands of German people from every city, town and village, young and old taking part with fervour and enthusiasm. A sea of hands raised in the Hitler salute, shouting *'Sieg Heil!'* They seemed in a trance, a mob ready to follow any order, no matter how criminal, and no matter what the consequences.

They sang their songs of hatred, and German domination and conquest of the whole world, and of spilling Jewish blood. I can still hear this stanza of another Hitler Youth song:

Wir werden weitermaschieren
Wenn alles in Trümmer fällt
Denn heute gehört uns Deutschland
Und morgen die ganze Welt.

(We shall continue to march on
Even if everything goes to ruin
For today Germany is ours
And tomorrow the whole world.)

How could they not have known when Jewish businesses and stores ceased to exist. When synagogues and Jewish buildings and Jewish schools were burnt and ransacked in front of their eyes. When Nazi thugs publicly beat Jewish men. When Jewish employees were not allowed to work with gentiles and consequently lost their jobs. When Jewish children were not permitted to attend state schools and universities any more. When notices posted on buildings, stores, cinemas, theatres and elsewhere proclaimed: 'Jews Not Welcome' (*Juden unerwünscht!*). When Jews had to wear the yellow star on their outer clothing and add 'Israel' or 'Sarah' to their names. When Jews were not allowed to use trains or other public transport to leave the villages and cities they lived in. When Jews were deported in cattle trucks. When some of their own, non-Jewish, prominent German political leaders, especially Social Democrats (Sozialdemokraten) and communists were openly murdered. When a number of courageous German intellectuals – writers, artists, educators, churchmen (like my grandmother's pastor) – lost their basic freedom, and often their lives, because they raised their voices in protest against the brutality and insanity that was sweeping over their land. The German people saw, they read, they heard, they knew. They did not want to admit that they saw and read and heard and knew.

But I also remember the two German soldiers who by refusing to send us back to Auschwitz and taking us instead to Merzdorf saved our lives, undoubtedly at considerable risk to themselves.

17 · My Child is Back!

I can no longer find any detailed notes describing our travel from Warburg to Lippborg, but I am reasonably sure that we arrived in Lippborg on 2 June, my father's birthday.

It was late in the afternoon, a beautiful sunny day. Lippborg has only one main street (Dorfstrasse). When we pushed our bikes up Dorfstrasse, I saw my mother in the middle of the street, carrying a large stack of clean washing on her way to my grandmother. I recognized her instantly. I had remembered her with black hair, but it had turned completely grey. When she saw us, she dropped the whole load of washing right there in the street. Tears were running down her cheeks. She looked at me and Buschi, and beyond. She stared down Dorfstrasse, her whole body seemed rigid. She turned back to us, and she realized that nobody else was with us. She embraced me and her first words were: 'Daddy and Bübchen [we called my brother Walter 'Bübchen'] are not coming back?' (*Papi und Bübchen kommen nicht zurück?*). She was crying and asking me a question and making a statement. She was shouting my Aunt Minchen's name. People came out of their houses. My mother kept repeating over and over, again and again: 'My child is back! My child is back!' (*Mein Kind ist zurück!*). My Aunt Minchen embraced me and cried and she kept asking: 'Where is Otto and Bübchen?' (*Wo ist Otto und Bübchen?*).

My Grandmother Schneider and Aunt Mille had been living in Lippborg for a year. The house they had lived in in Dortmund had been completely bombed out. They had found an apartment in the building of the local tavern on Dorfstrasse. So it was a wonderful surprise for me to see my grandmother and Aunt Mille walking up the street, I can still see the expression on my grandmother's face, and the tears running down her cheeks.

Poor Buschi knew that she was not coming back to Amsterdam to be received by any relatives. The Nazis had killed her non-Jewish husband; her parents were dead; she was an only child and she had to go back to Holland to her mother-in-law and father-in-law to tell them: 'I, the Jew, survived but your son perished in the camps.'

Buschi finally received her fully deserved attention from my mother, grandmother and aunts. We were bombarded with questions. The whole house was in turmoil. Aunt Minchen started to boil water in the large kettle for our baths and the zinc bathtub was placed on the tile floor in the big kitchen. My mother and Aunt Minchen gave us our baths while my grandmother was supervising the whole procedure with occasional helpful hints like: 'Use the brush around the neck, the feet need another going over!' My Aunt Mille went back to her apartment to start cooking. Our clothing was discarded, and my mother and my aunts found a whole array of suitable clothing for us to choose from.

My Aunts Luzi Schneider and Erna Schneider were also in Lippborg, their husbands Willi and Konrad were on their way back to Dortmund. Before my Aunt Luzi left, she tried to assure me that Uncle Willi 'really did not mean it', some years before, when he reproached my mother for marrying a Jew. I know that Aunt Luzi was not a Nazi, but I was unable to respond to the defence of her husband.*

When my Uncle Franz returned later from a trip to a neighbouring town, he found his house in a state of chaos. He gave us a great welcome. His mother, Mrs Nottelman, whom I have mentioned earlier, was also happy that we had returned. She was a pious old lady, and her room was full of crucifixes, pictures of Jesus and other religious symbols. My mother told me that she had prayed every night for our safe return.

We had to cover three years of separation. Every one of us was eager to learn what the other had gone through. I will start with my mother.

My mother had worked for the Schreyeck family in their leather factory in Düsseldorf, as I had mentioned earlier. The

---

*My Aunt Mille never forgave her brother Willi for uttering that reproach. She never spoke to him again and did not attend his funeral.

Gestapo made frequent visits to the factory after we were deported and questioned Mr Schreyeck about her. He eventually decided to send my mother to his factory in Vienna. He feared that it was not safe for her to remain in Düsseldorf because the Gestapo obviously had her under surveillance.

When the Gestapo appeared at the Vienna factory in the summer of 1944 to enquire about her whereabouts, it was fortunate that she was not at the factory at that time. The Schreyecks sent word to her to immediately leave Vienna. They asked her to take a train to Cleve, an industrial town near the Dutch border, where another Schreyeck brother had a tannery. My mother lived with and worked for the Cleve Schreyecks for a number of months. The Allied bombing raids were in full force at that time, and after a particularly bad bombing attack on that city, Mr and Mrs Schreyeck urged my mother to leave immediately for Lippborg, which she did. Their house took a direct hit that very night and both he and his wife perished.

When my mother came to Lippborg early in the winter of 1944, old Mrs Nottelmann, who had never allowed anybody to sleep in her room with her, offered to share it with my mother. My mother's brothers and their wives also spent some time in Lippborg to escape the bombs and the fighting at the end of the war. So Lippborg which had been belittled as the 'village in the sticks' (*das Kaff*), and which had been the subject of many family jokes, had become a refuge for the Schneider clan. Of course, Aunt Minchen provided food and shelter for all of them.

Buschi told my mother that she had vowed to bring me safely back to her and, since that had been accomplished, she was going to leave promptly for Holland. My mother and my aunt persuaded her to stay a while longer, so that she could rest and recuperate before facing the uncertainties awaiting her in Amsterdam. She slept at my grandmother and Aunt Mille's apartment, but she took all her meals with us at my Aunt Minchen's.

It was the strawberry season and Aunt Minchen had a huge berry garden. She and my mother claimed that Buschi and I spent a whole week in the garden, picking and eating berries. They were scrumptious. We had not seen never mind tasted a strawberry for years, so we had a feast. One day Uncle Franz asked my aunt why she had not baked any strawberry tarts. She winked at us and answered: 'This year the harvest is terrible, I cannot understand why!'

While people in the German cities were starving there was no food shortage at my aunt's. Uncle Franz made and repaired furniture. Many of his customers had prosperous, large farms which had not been damaged during the war. In lieu of payment they often gave him meat, butter, eggs, cheese and other farm products. (People regularly bartered during and after the war.)

My grandmother fulfilled my wish and made her famous jelly doughnuts (*Berliner Ballen*) for us. Food was still our foremost preoccupation. As a result of the rest and care and good food we started to gain weight, but several weeks later I felt somewhat bloated – in fact my whole body seemed rather swollen. It took almost two years for my system to get back to normal.

Buschi and I went for long walks together during which we tried to think about our future. I was very sure that I would not stay in Germany. I felt that I could never live a normal life there. I could not forget and I was not willing or ready to forgive. Buschi was not sure what she would do. She felt good about the Dutch people and would have been happy to have stayed in Holland for the rest of her life had her husband survived. As it was, she did not know her in-laws well and she felt very unsettled, alone and restless. She had to get back to Amsterdam to face her husband's parents. It was difficult for me to let her leave all by herself and it was hard to say goodbye. We promised each other that we would never lose touch, and we never did.

There were two additional rooms on the second floor of Aunt Minchen's house, but they had been rented to another couple. I had to sleep in Aunt Minchen and Uncle Franz's bedroom. This was a very large room with an extra wide double bed. Uncle Franz slept on one side, my aunt in the middle and I slept next to my aunt on the other side of the bed. My Aunt

118

Minchen was a very early riser, so very often Uncle Franz would still be sleeping on his side and I on mine. On a Sunday, the day after Buschi had left, my aunt was downstairs cooking breakfast, when Uncle Franz moved over to me and woke me up, embraced me and said: 'Be a little nice to Uncle Franz!' (*Sei doch mal nett zu Onkel Franz!*). I shot out of bed. He then implored me not to tell Aunt Minchen. He said that he really didn't mean anything. I was disgusted, but I was more concerned about my aunt, as I did not want to hurt her.

I told my mother about this only after we had left Lippborg, and we decided not to share it with anybody. As I mentioned before, Buschi had left the previous day, so I could give a sensible explanation to my aunt as to why I would now sleep at my grandmother's.

We had already spent days and nights relating our individual experiences. I wanted to know everything that had happened to each one of them since my deportation to Theresienstadt in July 1942. We cried a lot, but I was also learning to laugh again.

My Uncle Franz, as I have mentioned earlier, was a member of the SA (*Sturmabteilung* of the Nazi party, i.e. storm trooper). He owned a brown suit with a red swastika armband and all the other paraphernalia to complete his uniform, which was hanging in his wardobe. This 'monkey suit' (*Affenanzug*), as my aunt called his uniform, had been a bone of contention between them for years. He was a typical fellow traveller who did not 'approve' of 'everything' the Nazis did, but he wanted to be part of the club. His drinking companions – my aunt referred to them as his 'bar-room cronies' (*Saufkumpels*) – all belonged to the Nazi party. It was also good for business, he assured her. I remember their arguments about this long before I was deported into the camps. He would counter my aunt's objections with: 'You don't understand anything about this' (*Du verstehst ja nichts davon*).

The district SA leader, who lived in the village, was an old schoolmate of Uncle Franz's. He was a mean, shifty, corrupt colossus of a man, whose function consisted mainly of denouncing and threatening his fellow citizens. In early 1945 he questioned Uncle Franz about harbouring his 'Jew-loving sister-in-law' (*seine verjudete Schwägerin*), and warned him to get rid of her promptly. Everybody including my uncle was afraid of him, so it was remarkable when Uncle Franz countered with: ' She is going to remain in my house!' (*Die bleibt in meinem Haus!*). But I am also sure that my uncle would not have dared to disobey him prior to those closing months of the war.

My mother was in Lippborg when the American forces came into the village (probably mid-April 1945 – I am not sure of the exact date). According to my aunts and the accounts of others, the American tanks and trucks were driving up Dorfstrasse (the main street). The villagers had locked their doors and many went into hiding, including my Uncle Franz, who somehow did away with his uniform, and then crawled into the wardrobe, hiding under his suits and coats. He was scared to death. My aunt had warned him for years that this would happen, and now she was amused and made fun of the 'National Socialist heroes'. My mother told me she was not sure who welcomed the arrival of the 'Ammis' more (the Germans called the American forces 'Ammis'), she or my aunt.

The frightened village people watched the approaching army from their windows. The street was totally deserted, except for a grey-haired, 51-year-old woman, my mother, who walked toward them in the middle of the street, gesticulating and waving to them. My aunts and the other Schneider relatives, who were there at the time, were convinced that 'Lina' (as they called my mother) had gone mad. 'She is going to get shot or a tank will mow her down', they shouted.

The lead vehicle stopped, and my mother convinced them very quickly who she was. She was introduced to the officer in charge and he invited her into his jeep. Their first order of business was to round up the Nazis of the village. One of the officers spoke some Yiddish and others spoke some German, and so my mother became an important source of information to them. One of the officers was exceptionally kind to her, and supplied her with all kinds of food, chocolate and, the most important, coffee. She thought that he was Jewish, but that was mere conjecture on her part. She made sure that the district SA leader and some of his cohorts were the first ones to be arrested.

Of course, her dilemma was Uncle Franz. She must have painted him as an angel in a brown shirt because he eventually crawled out of his closet and escaped all punishment. As I write this, I can't help but feel that my mother must have experienced a bit of the satisfaction that Berthold Brecht's Jenny (of the *Threepenny Opera*) was fantasizing about.*

When I met my mother, I had the feeling she had feared that all three of us had perished. She kept touching me to convince herself that it was really me – something she would continue to do for a very long time. I wonder if the Americans entering the village had told her that the chances of seeing us again were not good. Some of these troops liberated concentration camps while they were advancing through Germany.

Once in a while she would say to me: 'You think that somehow they could have survived?', and she would immediately answer it herself with: 'I know, no use talking about it, it won't bring them back.' She would cry so bitterly that her whole body would shake and I did not know how to console her.

---

*Since Uncle Franz had financially overextended himself he went into bankruptcy sometime after the end of the war – he lost his factory and his house. My mother and her second husband Siegmund gave them as much financial help as they were able to muster. As far as I know, few if any relatives who found safe haven and food at his and my aunt's house during the war, were able or willing to come to their aid. Uncle Franz died in 1968.

18 · Düsseldorf Again

My mother and I felt it was time to travel to Düsseldorf, where we hoped to find some news about our relatives, and make plans and decisions concerning our future. After tearful goodbyes, we managed to get a ride in a truck to a small town called Beckum, not too far from Lippborg. (Lippborg did not have a railway station.)

Anybody attempting to travel in Germany by train in June 1945 had to be resigned to spending days, and very often nights, at railway stations just waiting and hoping to catch whatever passenger or freight train might happen to come along, only to discover that it was not going where one thought or was told it would go. Many damaged railway bridges were still impassable. Very few trains were running, and those that did were terribly overcrowded. People were literally hanging from doors and windows. We had little luggage as my mother had lost practically everything. We did catch a train (we had to change a few times), and we did some hitchhiking and a lot of walking, but eventually we reached Düsseldorf.

My mother knew a family called Winkens in Gerresheim, a suburb of Düsseldorf (she had made friends with them after our deportation). Mr Theo Winkens was not Jewish (he was a member of the Seventh Day Adventists), but his wife was Jewish. They had no children. When the Gestapo wanted to deport her, he managed to hide her and save her life.

They owned their own house, one of a number of terraced houses arranged in a continuous line, which formed part of a development. He built a false wall in their basement, behind which he had built a tiny room without windows (the entrance of this room was very cleverly camouflaged). Mrs Winkens did not see daylight during the whole time she spent in her hideout. When the Gestapo came to his house to arrest his wife, he assured them that she had run away and that he was glad to be finally rid of her. Sometimes he would bring her up at night, in complete darkness. Occasionally he would invite German women to his house, making sure that he was seen in their company.

The Winkens welcomed us into their house, and they insisted that we stay with them as long as we needed to. Mr Winkens and a few of his close friends, some of them probably communists, conducted a determined campaign to seek out Nazis, especially those who had lived in confiscated Jewish property.

Theo Winkens had a crippled arm from an injury he had suffered during World War I. His country gave him the Iron Cross, first class, in gratitude. (This is the highest distinction a German soldier could receive during that war.) He was a pastry chef and biscuit-baker by trade. He was of medium height and build, with a fair complexion and reddish hair. His wife had health problems when I met her. She was heavily built, with an olive complexion, and her eyes protruding, as they often do in people who suffer from a thyroid condition.

Theo Winkens' new official position involved seizure of Nazi property including possessions and properties the Nazis had 'confiscated' – a better word is stolen – from the 'enemies of the Reich', in other words, Jews and the victims of political persecution.

Mr Winkens found us a nice apartment, one of three family-sized apartments in a house which had been formerly occupied by a Nazi functionary, who had taken it from the original Jewish owner when he was deported to a camp. The house was located fairly close to the Winkens. When the former Nazi occupants fled, they left most of their belongings and furniture behind. This was very convenient for us, but neither my mother nor I considered this loot as something we wanted to keep. Our stay was strictly temporary. We wanted to leave Germany – the sooner the better.

As I mentioned earlier, my father's last attempt to earn a living in Nazi Germany was a wholesale business which he opened on Karlstrasse in Düsseldorf and successfully ran until the Nazis forced all Jews to 'sell' their businesses. My mother had become friendly with a door-to-door saleswoman who was a customer of theirs. This woman convinced my mother that she hated the Nazis. They kept in touch after my father had to divest himself of the business and after our deportation to Theresienstadt.

When my mother had to give up her apartment and leave Düsseldorf in a hurry, this woman offered to save our dining room furniture for her – the last pieces of decent furniture my mother owned. My mother had also entrusted her with the safe keeping of some rings. The woman lived a good distance from the city in a very humble setting, in what the Germans call '*Schrebergärten*'. (Poor people were given land allotments and they would usually build their own shack with a vegetable garden surrounding it. Most of these houses were fairly primitively constructed.)

My mother visited this woman in 1944, probably on her way from Vienna to Cleve, to ask for her rings, which she needed to sell because she was very short of money. Her 'good friend' opened the door, did not invite her in and sarcastically asked: 'What do you want here?' She answered my mother's request with: 'I don't have anything of yours, you Jewish bitch; get out of here and don't you ever dare to come back or I'll see to it that you get locked up!' (*Sonst sorge ich dafür dass Sie auf Numero Sicher kommen!*). My mother could see her dining room furniture through the open door before that door was slammed shut in her face.

Theo Winkens made it a top priority to visit this lady with my mother and his assistants. They drove there in a large truck. He showed his credentials when she opened the door, and they unceremoniously loaded the dining room furniture on to the truck. He then asked for the rings, which she instantly surrendered. He left her and her boyfriend shaken, with the distinct impression that he was not finished with her yet. This little bit of justice rendered made my mother feel good. She only took back what was hers in the first place, but ironically she was to leave the dining room furniture in Düsseldorf. She had regained something that she would never have use for again.

One of our first visits was to the newly established offices of the Jewish Congregation. A couple were running the operation at that time: he was Jewish and she was from a non-Jewish background. Except for some Jewish men who had managed to save themselves through their marriage to non-Jewish partners, such as my Uncle Erich and Paul Cohen, there were practically no German Jews left. They had either emigrated or they had been murdered. Very few survivors like myself even tried to return to their home towns. They usually waited in Displaced Persons' Camps for their chance to emigrate to Palestine or the United States. Some tried to enter Palestine illegally via Italy.

I had hoped for some news of the fate of my relatives and friends; that was my main reason for going there. I soon realized that they knew less than I did. I met a tall, burly man who introduced himself as 'Dr Auerbach', he left me with the impression that he was a prominent Jewish leader who had survived the concentration camps. He was a gifted orator, oozing self-confidence and displaying an aura of leadership. He promised help to people like myself and hinted at his many important connections. I wondered why he had returned to Germany and why he had chosen Düsseldorf, since it was not his home town and he had no family there.

He later left that city to assume an influential position in the Bavarian Government. His mercurial ascent collapsed some time later when he was exposed as a former *Kapo*. (As I have mentioned earlier *Kapos* were inmates chosen by the SS to serve as their stooges for policing, and they often brutally beat and punished their fellow prisoners.) Shortly after he was exposed, 'Dr Auerbach' committed suicide.

Of course, we needed money to support ourselves, and so I decided to give English language lessons. My advertisements bore fruit, and I ended up with a fair number of adult students who came to our apartment for lessons. I enjoyed the challenge of teaching.

Shortly after I had started my language school, I received a visitor who identified himself as a Ukrainian who had been living in Germany. He emphasized his language expertise and his university education, though his German did not testify to his claims. He said that he spoke many languages, and also that he had a language school, teaching everything from Russian to English, including Spanish and more. Did I realize that I had to be licensed to teach, he asked me. Maybe I would work for him, he suggested. I declined the invitation.

My teaching career came to an abrupt halt, only days after this man's visit, when I was asked to appear at the English Military Headquarters to see Captain Plum. When I entered Captain Plum's office, I realized that the American and English military had a lot in common. Captain Plum received me sitting at his desk with his feet resting on it. He called out: 'Hello', never moving from his position, and pointed to a chair for me to sit on. I was quite nervous as I had no idea why I had been summoned to his office.

He was very nice to me and he enquired about my experiences during the war. He then questioned me about my intentions and future plans. I was wondering: 'Is this why he asked me to see him?' He advised me to seek help from international and Jewish organizations for refugees such as the United Nations Relief and Rehabilitation Administration (UNRRA) and to go to a displaced persons' camp. 'That would be by far the best way to get into the United States', he said. He kept emphasizing that he did not know the proper procedures to accomplish this, but from what he had heard, these organizations would be helpful to people in my situation. I could not believe that that was all he had on his mind. I told him that I appreciated his concern and that I would follow his advice. He wished me well and had almost dismissed me, but when I had just about reached the door, he said: 'By the way, Miss Lenneberg, this Ukrainian person who runs a language school, do you know him? He denounced you to us because you teach without a licence. Don't teach anymore, there is no future for you in that anyway. Think about my suggestions, and good luck to you and your mother!'

When I entered the reception area after leaving Captain Plum's office, I recognized my father's cousin Paul Kohn in the waiting area. He had returned from Holland where he had been hiding. (I mentioned him earlier: he was married to my Aunt Erna Lenneberg's sister Maria.) I ran to him. 'Hello Uncle Paul,' I said. He seemed preoccupied and nervous, and barely returned my greeting. He never enquired about my father and my brother, or for that matter about my mother or me. He had more important things on his mind. He was apparently pursuing restitution of the Kohn properties and store. I felt hurt and disgusted by his behaviour. Captain Plum's words still echoed in my brain. Leaving Germany became an obsession.

Shortly after arriving in Düsseldorf I met a Canadian officer. He had visited the Jewish community offices and asked to be introduced to a Jewish girl. He invited me to the officers' club. I enjoyed meeting people my own age. I liked to converse in English and I also enjoyed dancing. This new social life was very good for me. I regained my self-confidence and I had some fun. We dated often and I liked him. He was good-looking, tall and trim. He had blue eyes and blondish curly hair. He was considerate and charming and attentive to my mother. He would pick me up in his stylish military car, and he included me in social gatherings and outings with his fellow officers and their German girlfriends. I felt oddly out of place on occasions, although it seems rather strange to me now, but at the time I enjoyed being part of the social mix.

19 · Struggle to Leave Germany

Shortly after my conversation with Captain Plum, I decided to travel to Munich alone, to seek help from the United Nations Relief and Rehabilitation Administration (UNRRA) and American Joint Distribution Committee (AJDC) and Hebrew Immigrant Aid Society (HIAS) to obtain an affidavit, and then hopefully visas for my mother and me to enter the United States.

It was not easy to get to Munich. Large stretches of rail lines were still out of action. Very few trains were running and those that were, were very crowded; connections were abysmal and in some cases non-existent. People were literally hanging out of windows and doors.

After visiting several agencies and the American Consulate in Munich it became clear that we could have a long wait ahead of us, but the good news was that we qualified to be included on a collective affidavit sponsored by one of the Jewish agencies.

Munich, like most German cities after the war, had a terrible shortage of housing, so I was fortunate to find a furnished room with a widowed lady who let me cook my meals in her kitchen. I also visited the offices of Dr Auerbach, who at that time held an influential position in the Bavarian Government as a privy councillor (*Regierungsrat*). He was a very busy man. While he was storming through his offices he acknowledged my existence with a wave of his hand and without perceptibly slowing down he told his secretary: 'Please find a job here for Fräulein Lenneberg.' My typing and shorthand skills were quite inadequate so I felt totally out of place. I only worked there for a brief period of time.

In spite of my aversion to camps, I finally heeded Captain Plum's advice and travelled to Deggendorf, a displaced persons' (DP) camp in Bavaria, about 80 miles northeast of Munich on the River Danube (Donau) at the edge of the Bavarian Forest. I found some of my friends from Theresienstadt there, among them my former colleague Trude's parents. They were eager to welcome us and they were indeed very helpful.

I worried about subjecting my mother to this awful train trip, but it all worked out and we took up residence in Deggendorf. We were assigned a spacious room in a large villa, which was used as the school, in the camp's grounds. My Theresienstadt friends had some influence and they took good care of us. I gave English language lessons to children and adults. My mother made friends very quickly and she adjusted well to camp life, contrary to my expectations and fears.

We were able to do our own cooking and housekeeping. The house we lived in served as the school building for the camp's children. A non-Jewish Estonian woman who worked for UNRRA as an interpreter occupied another room in the building. Unfortunately, we had to share the bathroom with her, and she was not fastidious. She usually left the bathtub encrusted with greasy black rings, and she made it obvious that she did not welcome our presence in the house. She used the bathtub to wash her clothes and dishes, sometimes occupying the bathroom for hours. She showed no interest in us. She was very secretive and we could not help but wonder where and how she had spent the war years. Fortunately she was not present during the day. The best one could say was that we tolerated each other.

Most camp-dwellers had few or no identification papers except for those issued by UNRRA for each resident of the camp. These papers were mainly based on statements made to the UNRRA authorities by each individual who lived in the camp. Almost everybody in a DP camp wanted to immigrate somewhere so, for example, they needed papers to testify to their wartime activities or imprisonment, and documents to verify their date and place of birth.

Buschi and I had already experienced first-hand how much a piece of paper with an official-looking stamp could mean to one's ability to move freely, and how at times it could mean the difference between life and death.

The office (a room in the Deggendorf camp) of the notary, Herr Notar Tuch, could have been the setting of a comic opera. 'Herr Notar', as we called him, was a tall, slender, mild-mannered, bespectacled middle-aged man with a serious official bearing. He was totally aware of his important standing in the camp community. He had an old typewriter, badly in need of repair, on which he typed (I think only with two fingers) uncountable affidavits and sworn statements (*Eidesstattliche Erklärungen*) composed in longwinded, convoluted style, each one signed by witnesses who had to swear to its veracity.

His overworked secretary, another camp resident, would sometimes share his office. She carried an important-looking file and shorthand notebook to take down Herr Notar's voluminous verbose dictations. His German was a mixture of Austrian German and the phrasing frequently used by Polish Jews. It all sounded very official and bore the stamp of DP Camp Deggendorf. We were taken to Herr Notar, and my mother and I ended up with a fistful of sworn statements attested and sworn to by my friends.

Waiting for our turn to receive our visas took longer than we had expected, but my mother never complained and gladly adjusted to collective living because she saw hope and a future for us in the United States. Life in Germany was intolerable for her: she was constantly reminded of years spent in that land in utter desperation and fear, ultimately ending with the greatest loss one can suffer.

Whilst in Deggendorf I befriended Lodzia, a bright and lovely young woman. Lodzia was born in Poland, and she too had survived the camps. We had a lot in common: we laughed, we had fun, we talked and dreamed together. I wish that we had stayed in touch. (I think she probably emigrated to Palestine.) I also became friendly with Leon Feigenblatt. Leon had survived the camps and he had no family left. Both Lodzia and Leon spent a lot of time with us in our 'luxurious' (by Deggendorf standards) accommodation. My mother listened to their stories, cooked for them, and gave love and understanding to all of us.

Leon was determined to go to Palestine. He had returned from Italy, where he had been unsuccessful in obtaining a passage to Palestine. He was upset about the terrorist acts which the Irgun had perpetrated there. Irgun Zvai Leumi was a group which used violence to force the British to allow all Jews, especially the survivors of the Holocaust, to enter Palestine. He felt strongly that it was unfair to Italy, which was providing a safe haven for many Jews waiting to go to Palestine. Many blamed the British for the whole dilemma – people were desperate and many lost their lives trying to reach Palestine after they survived Hitler's camps.

Leon and I spent a lot of time together, but we had each decided on different countries in which to start anew. There was no future for us together and we both accepted that. I made frequent trips to Munich to check on our immigration status, and he sometimes accompanied me there. I hope he reached Palestine and that he has had a full and good life in Israel.

On one such trip to Munich I ran into Kurt Rosenbaum, who had worked with me in Theresienstadt in the Youth Home of L414. He was working for the American Joint Distribution Committee, and I almost did not recognize him. He wore an American uniform, which was of course most unusual for a recently liberated survivor of the Nazi camps. I have no explanation as to how he had managed to obtain his position. I was happy to see him alive and well. (Sadly, his whole family had perished.) I was looking forward to a reunion with the Kurt I remembered from L414 but, alas, the smart handsome young man I faced was a stranger to me. The compliments he paid me, and his language and mannerisms, were a copy of a GI trying to pick up a girl. I told him that I had business to attend to at the AJDC regarding our immigration, whereupon he directed me to a door of an office, instructing me to call him after I was finished, adding that I could spend the night at his apartment. I never saw the apartment. I never saw Kurt again.

On one occasion we had to go to the DP camp in Passau. We

needed to obtain an official UNRRA paper which was unavailable in Deggendorf. Passau is a town about a hundred miles northeast of Munich and 30 miles southeast of Deggendorf, situated near the Austrian border. We were able to catch a train to Passau. A farmer gave us a lift from the railway station to the DP camp in his horse-drawn open wagon. The surrounding countryside was breathtakingly beautiful, with lush green valleys and meadows fringed by a rugged mountain chain.

This camp, one of the larger ones in Bavaria, had among others a population of Jews from an Orthodox sect. The men wore their traditional long black coats, black hats and sidecurls, while the women had kerchiefs and long dresses. These people were intolerant of their fellow Jewish survivors, condemning their non-religious brothers and sisters and refusing to recognize them as Jews. They were a close-knit group and they showed no consideration for anybody who did not subscribe to their life-style. They were involved in trading everything one could think of, from herring, to gold and diamonds, to American dollars.

As we walked through the camp, we were surprised to see that they had entirely taken over many roads. They had set up boxes and crates in the lanes, on the grass – wherever they felt like peddling their wares. The business was conducted by men only. We saw one man dishing out herring, its juices running down his kaftan-like coat and sleeves. Others had congregated around their bags and boxes gesticulating and noisily conversing, completely blocking the road, totally oblivious that other people or vehicles might want to pass. They were solely involved with themselves, lacking any regard for anybody outside their group.

We met an Australian Jewish physician who was working at the UNRRA Headquarters there. He complained bitterly about the difficulties these people were creating for everybody. He added: 'They are impossible to deal with and impossible to live with. They have no concept of hygiene. Their women are treated like subordinate creatures. Their living standards are centuries removed from ours!' We had gleaned a glimpse of their life and manners, and it would have been impossible for us to have coexisted with them even for a limited time. We were quite ready to return to Deggendorf. Coming from Passau, it was almost like coming home.

During this time, Buschi and I corresponded faithfully. She had visited her in-laws, who were of course devastated by her news that their son had perished. She did not feel at ease with them, and she had decided to live by herself after securing employment as a nanny.

Literature and the arts had always been part of her life, and fortunately she met people with similar interests with whom she made friends. She entered into a relationship with an artist of independent means. She lived with him, but though he was kind and considerate to her and they shared the same interests and tastes it did not work out for them. Eventually she decided to leave Europe and to seek immigration to the United States.

I heard from Buschi shortly before we left Deggendorf; by that time neither one of us had heard from our Czech friends. We thought a lot about Hannah, and we worried as to whether or not she had survived her heart attack.

My mother met Mrs Roth in Deggendorf. They were the same age, and Mrs Roth had also lost her husband, and her two sons. (I think she originally came from Warsaw.) The two women became close friends: they shared their grief and their hopes and were inseparable. My mother learned many Yiddish expressions from Mrs Roth. She would often mispronounce or misapply them, and the results were hilarious. My friends Lodzia and Leon teased her a lot, which did not faze her in the least. After she learned that in Yiddish a needle is a '*Nudel*' (in German *Nudel* means noodle), and in Yiddish a noodle is a '*nadel*' (*Nadel* is the German word for needle), she announced – literally shaking with laughter – that she was serving '*Nadel Suppe*' (needle soup) for dinner!

Mrs Roth also wanted to emigrate to the United States, but the Polish quota was much smaller than the German quota, so her waiting period was considerably longer than ours. US law had set quotas for each country of origin (defined as the country of birth). The German quota was the most favourable, because few German-born Jews had survived, and many Germans were afraid to be scrutinized about their former political (that is, Nazi) affiliations, and therefore visa applications for that segment of the population must have been miniscule. Still, a sizeable number of German war-brides were immigrating into the United States.

Many Polish refugees pretended to be German-born in order to go to the United States. The consulate was aware of this, and started to scrutinize prospective immigrants more closely, quizzing them in detail about the town in which they claimed to have been born. Most Polish-born Jews who spoke German, spoke it with an easily detectable accent. Anyone caught misrepresenting his place of birth would ruin forever his chances of entering the United States. Many people desperately wanted to leave the camps, and foolishly tried to deceive the American consular officials. Some succeeded, but only because their German was good or because they could claim that their place of birth was situated in border areas which had been part of Germany. They also had to convince the consul that they could not obtain a copy of their birth certificate.

There was a flourishing black market where one could buy forged papers of any description which, instead of being useful, got many people into endless trouble. At best, it caused even longer delays and, at worst, could result in complete denial of an entry visa to the United States.

The camp was rife with rumours and insinuations about encounters at the US consulate. Somebody had heard that there was a new consul who asked all kinds of questions about street names and important landmarks of the German town one was born in, and whose manner of questioning was purposely confusing! This or that secretary was particularly nasty. The doctor reading the chest x-ray would see something untoward on every x-ray he took! And so on it went.

I worried about possible scars in my lungs from my bout with scrofula (TB of the lymph nodes) which I had contracted as a child. My mother had suffered from gallbladder problems since the birth of my brother, and during the last years she had experienced a few nasty attacks. Not surprisingly, when we were finally summoned to appear before the consul in Munich we were both nervous wrecks. Fortunately, my Uncle Konrad lived in Dortmund and was able to obtain copies of our birth certificates, which he sent to us just in time before we left for Munich. This made things a little easier for us.

I believe we left Deggendorf sometime towards the end of May 1947. We had to arrange transport for ourselves and our luggage to the 'Funk Kaserne', a large complex of former military barracks in Munich which housed DPs in transit to the United States. We stayed here while undergoing medical tests and waiting for our interview with the consul. I was able to organize a large open truck to take us and a number of other residents of the camp who had also received notification to appear at the consulate. Among them was Mrs Erna Goldschmidt and her son and daughter (Jochem, sixteen and Eva, seventeen), also the Gellers. (Mr Geller was still addressed as 'Panje Ingenieure' – Mr Engineer. I particularly remember a young, newly wed couple, Netka and Leon Geldzähler, who were so much in love with each other. We were very fond of them. They had survived the camps, though they had lost their families. They felt a bond with my mother whose love and caring sustained many of us.

At the Funk Kaserne we had to produce more forms, such as a medical history and additional supporting documents, including birth certificates, statements of good conduct from the police, identification papers from the UNRRA and from the Deggendorf camp authorities. We also had to submit to extensive physical examinations and chest X-rays. Even our toenails and fingernails were inspected for fungal infection. My mother and I had been put on a collective affidavit by the AJDC. Daily lists were posted on the barrack bulletin boards showing the names of people who were to see the consul, giving the time and date; a second list showed the names of people who had to present themselves to be X-rayed, re-examined or re-X-rayed. There were other lists naming people who lacked documents, and, of course, the most important list was the one that bore the names of people who had been awarded visas.

I found my name on the second list. I had to make a repeat appearance at the medical department of the consulate to be re-X-rayed. Of course, I was terribly worried because of my scrofula history. So much depended upon the results of this X-ray. 'Waiting' was the name of the game! I had to wait for hours to be X-rayed, and we had to wait hours whenever we had to appear for whatever reason.

At the Funk Kaserne we and our Deggendorf friends would frequently take turns checking the bulletin boards for any new listing of names. Someone spotted our names among the people scheduled to appear before the consul. We were elated: my chest X-ray obviously had been diagnosed as negative for TB.

We were sitting in the waiting area outside the consul's chambers when my mother's name was called out by his secretary – a small, middle-aged, severe-looking woman. The consul was very civilized in his manner of questioning my mother. He did ask her, after she thought he had finished with her – and obviously this was his technique to catch people off guard – 'So where did you say your husband was?' Her response, and the manner in which she reacted, must have convinced him that she was speaking the truth. His questioning of me was straightforward, and we both passed his scrutiny without any problem. It was apparent that the consul made frequent eye-contact with his secretary. Her approval evidently was an important factor in his decision-making.

Some of our former Deggendorf fellow residents were not so lucky. They encountered long delays and an extended stay at the Funk Kaserne.

My mother and I eagerly and excitedly read the notice on the bulletin board that Franziska Karoline Lenneberg and Ursula Lenneberg were among the people listed to present themselves with their luggage at the appointed date and time in a designated area of the barracks, to receive instruction for transport to Bremen. Trucks duly brought us and our luggage to the railway station, where we boarded a freight train. I think we arrived in Bremen during the very last days of May 1947.

20 · Ship to New York

After our arrival in Bremen we were transferred to another transit camp in Bremerhaven. We had only been there for a very short time, when my mother developed chills and fever, nausea and abdominal pain. We were both panic-stricken. We had come this far, and we had just learned that our names had been placed on the passenger list of the SS *Ernie Pyle*, a World War II transport ship which was to leave a few days hence.

My mother received help at the local US military hospital and made a good recovery. A young American doctor diagnosed an acutely inflamed gall-bladder. He treated her with an antibiotic (I think it was penicillin) and put her on a fat-free diet. He stressed that she needed immediate medical attention in the United States. He added: 'If the immigration people find out that you have an acute gallbladder condition, they will not allow you to board ship. Don't talk to anybody about my diagnosis until you get into the States! No fatty foods! Good luck and *bon voyage!*'

We were fortunate that my mother was treated at a US medical facility. German hospitals did not have antibiotics like penicillin readily available, and were very short of doctors. In pre-Nazi Germany many of the most capable doctors and professors at medical schools had been Jews. Subsequently, they had either emigrated or been murdered by the Nazis. (Of course, many non-Jewish doctors had been killed in the war.)

The Goldschmidts, who had been held up in Munich because of some medical questions, finally received their visa too, and we met them again in Bremerhaven. They were scheduled to leave on the next ship following ours.

We took a few trips into Bremen and Bremerhaven, and I

remember that we bought delicious smoked fish from a peddler at a street corner. He had a large, open metal drum with smoky smouldering chips of wood: the fish were placed over it on top of an iron grate. The savory aroma permeated the whole neighbourhood.

The most wonderful surprise awaited us on the day before our embarkation when my grandmother, Aunt Minchen and Aunt Mille arrived in Bremerhaven to see us off. My grandmother cried and in her matter of fact way told me: 'Urselchen, you'll never see your Oma again. America is so far away, and I am too old to cross that huge ocean!' Even though she lived to the age of 96 (she died in 1963) I never did see her again.

We had waited so long for this day. The five of us were standing at the quay, admiring this relatively small, 12,000 ton troop transport ship which looked huge to us. (I don't think the *Queen Mary* could have impressed us more!) We heard the sailors shouting in English, busy getting the ship ready for boarding. The pier was crowded with people and their luggage. Everybody was talking, it seemed, at the same time, in many different languages. Some were determined to be the first on board. They started squeezing and pushing, but eventually even they realized that their berths had been preassigned.

Some of our fellow passengers were refugees from DP camps like us: people of many different nationalities, most of them Jews. There were a fair number of German war-brides among the passengers, and some Germans who were partly Jewish.

It was our turn to pass through the last inspection before boarding the ship. One last embrace and kiss. All five of us were in tears. I can still see them standing on the quay: my tiny grandmother, standing there almost limp, flanked by my aunts. They stood there for a very long time waving and dabbing their eyes.

We followed the people in line ahead of us and eventually found ourselves on the boat. At that moment I was not consciously aware that I was taking a momentous step into the future course of my life. My mother and I stood on the top deck of the SS *Ernie Pyle* waving back to our family. They looked so small and already so far away.*

On deck we were greeted by the captain and his crew, including the kitchen personnel, all decked out in their clean white uniforms. It seemed to me that the majority of the crew were black. I had never seen a black person before I was deported into the camps. It was only after my liberation when we had entered the American-occupied zone of Germany that I saw black American soldiers. As a persecuted young person in Germany I felt an affinity with black people, especially after I had read *Uncle Tom's Cabin* (*Onkel Tom's Hütte*). Their history and my persecution had a common thread. It was the same feeling I had had when I was loading flax at the railway siding in Merzdorf and English prisoners of war marched past us.

I had never travelled anywhere on a large boat before, it was all strange and exciting, and a bit overwhelming for me. My mother and I were assigned different cabins, which upset us at first, but we soon discovered that we could spend as much time together as we wished and it really did not bother us at all.

I was welcomed by my steward on deck 'C', my cabin number was 52 and I was given bed No. 3. I shared the cabin with 25 other women. Most of them were complaining bitterly about the crowded conditions. They thought it was 'horrible' (*fürchterlich*), but it did not upset me at all. (Perhaps I did not forget the past as quickly as some of my cabin mates!)

My mother and I went up on the main deck from where we watched life on the pier. People were hurrying along, loaded down with bags and packages; suitcases and valises were still being loaded on to the ship. After two and a half hours of intensive labour by the crew, and a lot of hustling and bustling, the SS *Ernie Pyle* was leaving Bremerhaven.

---

*My mother travelled to Germany once a year to see her sisters (Aunt Minchen and Aunt Mille). Aunt Minchen had gone blind because of a neglected glaucoma and cataract condition. My mother took her to a university clinic in Germany, where late surgical intervention restored some minimal vision.

I am grateful that I visited my aunts with my husband and my two sons in the early summer of 1975. It was the last time I saw Aunt Minchen. She was still living in Lippborg, and died in November of that year aged 83.

Aunt Mille was visiting us in the United States in 1978 when she had to undergo emergency surgery for rectal cancer. She died in Germany in 1980, aged 73.

It was 4.30 p.m. on Friday, 13 June 1947, and we were on board! All 900 passengers were pressing close to the railings to watch as the sailors were retracting the landing stage. They untied the ropes. Small motorized boats were pulling us away from the pier. The engines were thumping. We were leaving Germany, we were leaving Europe. We were on our way to the United States.

Of course my first order of business was to inspect our new accommodation – our home for the next ten days. I checked out every nook and cranny of the boat. The engineer proudly showed me the large engines which were hard at work. The oil smell and noise level were overpowering. The cabins all looked alike, crammed full of tightly packed passengers. The self-service cafeteria was clean and inviting; however, the lounge and room set aside for reading and socializing were rather primitive and small. My favourite place was the main deck; I spent very little time in my cabin.

The ship's course took us into the North Sea. Even in June it was very rough, and already a few of our passengers were seasick. It started with a few who were throwing up, but spread rapidly like an epidemic, and I decided to stay on the main deck. I even slept in the lounge since the stench and moaning and groaning in my cabin was unbearable.

On 14 June we sighted the coast of Dover. By that time 75 per cent of the passengers were seasick. I did not feel any ill effects during the voyage; on the contrary, I felt great. My mother was also surrounded by vomiting cabin mates, so I coaxed her out of her bunk and brought her into fresh air. I gave her an aspirin, and told her that it was medication given to me by the ship's surgeon guaranteed to prevent seasickness. She was convinced of its effectiveness as anything that came from America had to be good! Indeed it worked for her. I am sure it helped to keep her on the main deck in fresh air, away from her vomit-covered cabin, but since then I have never doubted the psychological value of placebos.

During the morning of 14 June I met a young man on the main deck. He introduced himself as Albert Eising from Munich. He told me that he was half-Jewish. (I thought that I remembered seeing an attractive young lady seeing him off at the pier. We enjoyed each other's company, and we found a lot to talk about. My mother claimed that she did not see me for ten days! I cannot remember whether Albert Eising was engaged or married to this young woman who took leave from him when we were boarding the ship, but it did not matter to me. We had a good time together. We enjoyed the passage and each other's company, but I had no intention of becoming seriously involved with him. It seems so strange to me now that we spent so much time together but we never departed from speaking to each other in the formal German *Sie*. He would address me as 'Fräulein Lenneberg' and I would counter with 'Herr Eising'.

So many people were unwell that the cafeteria was almost completely deserted. The good sailors amongst us were receiving wonderful service, excellent food and plenty of attention from the friendly crew. Our favourite mess steward gave us wonderful oranges and delightful cookies. We loved the snow-white bread, which tasted like cake to us, topped with delicious butter. We were enjoying food which we had not seen for years. It was not always easy to eat though, and I remember one meal when the sea was so rough that dishes and food were sliding off the tables. It seemed that the ship was riding the waves in a semi-vertical rather than horizontal plane. It was exciting to watch the swelling and ebbing of the huge waves. At times I was convinced that we would all be washed overboard by the mountains of moving water approaching us, but fortunately our boat managed to stay on top of them. As we entered calmer waters I watched exotic fish speeding by. The air temperature was much warmer now and there was nothing but the great ocean as far as our eyes could see.

One morning the friendly steward told us that we should be approaching New York Harbor in three days. For a week we had been living without a care on this boat, but in three days we would have to face a new life, and I tried to speculate what that would be like. I knew that my mother would find it difficult to communicate, as her knowledge of English was very limited. I felt uneasy about her health, particularly her repeated gall-bladder attacks, but in spite of these concerns I was optimistic that somehow it would all be made right once we were in the United States. I knew that it would not be easy for my mother, at 52, to adjust to a new culture. How, I wondered, would she earn a living? In spite of my trepidation, I was confident that we would cope. I think that my enthusiasm and self-assurance inspired her to muster the will and strength and determination needed to do her part to make a new life for ourselves. She relied on me and she trusted me. It was natural for me to assume responsibility for both of us. Soon we would step on the soil of a land that my parents and my brother and I had tried to reach more than nine long years ago.

As we were approaching New York Harbor we saw the Statue of Liberty. We felt that she was extending a special welcome to us – as I am sure many immigrants must have felt before us. It was an indescribable emotional experience. With tears running down her cheeks, my mother said to me: 'We have paid our debt – I think life here will only have good things in store for us!' We were passing by the 'beautiful lady' with her outstretched hands when the New York skyline came into view with its multiple skyscrapers. Everybody was on deck, talking, gesticulating, waving – and sweating. New York welcomed us on a very hot, muggy June day. My mother turned to me with some alarm in her voice: 'O God, that's the American heat!' (*Mein Gott, dass ist die Amerikanische Hitze.*)

The SS *Ernie Pyle* was now docked at one of the lower Manhattan piers. A number of immigration officials with briefcases and stacks of papers were boarding our ship. Each passenger was individually called out to be interviewed by these officials. Some were asked about their medical history, many got their papers very promptly and were then allowed to leave the boat.

My mother received her papers and permission to disembark. Of course, she waited for me since I had not been called yet. We were both getting concerned: why had there been no mention at all of my name? Could there be some mistake? Could my papers have got lost? (My mother's and my papers had always been together.)

I was the last passenger to be summoned. They asked me to go into one of the cabins on the main deck. Several doctors were seated around a large table which was covered with piles of papers. One of the older doctors, who was handling my medical records, questioned me about my scrofula infection when I was six years old. He mentioned that he was not at all familiar with this type of tuberculosis. He asked me: 'Did you ever have active TB? Did it ever affect your lungs?' My response was 'no', but I added that I had been X-rayed twice at the consulate in Munich, and that I had been given a clean bill of health. He consulted another physician, and then he asked me about the scar and the calcified lymph nodes in my neck which were the result of the original infection. Neither of these learned gentlemen was inclined to let me into the country. At that point the youngest physician of that group spoke up and educated his older colleagues about the nature of this disease called 'scrofula'; he then added: 'As a result of it she probably has more immunity to TB than any one of us!' At last I received my entry papers! My mother and I were the last passengers to leave the SS *Ernie Pyle*.

21 · Hotel Marseille

It was 23 June 1947, a little past noon, and my mother and I were following the signs through deserted passage-ways when we entered a huge hall at the pier. It had the appearance of a small indoor arena with a sort of visitors' gallery, where the names of arriving passengers were called out when they entered the hall. It was here that the new arrivals were picked up by relatives and friends. We had been delayed for such a long time that almost all the other passengers had already left, so the place was practically deserted except for a short thickset gentleman in his early fifties wearing a panama hat. He called out our name after it had been announced on the loudspeaker and greeted us very warmly. What a surprise! We had not had any communication with Victor Adler and his wife Bessie, distant relatives of my father's, since they had left Düsseldorf, probably around 1937 or 1938. I cannot recall how he was notified of our arrival.

Our sponsor, AJDC, had reserved rooms at the Hotel Marseille on Broadway in Manhattan for immigrants without family able to take them in. Victor took us in his (what seemed to us) enormously large luxurious automobile and drove us to the Hotel Marseille.

During the car ride I was craning my neck to take in the sights of this enormous city. All these different people! Some blond with light complexions, others with dark and olive skin; black people in light suits and panama hats. People rushing by in cars, on foot, on bicycles. Stores with their wares on the pavements. Carts with fruit and drinks and hot dog vendors. Large advertisements everywhere. A big billboard with a fellow actually smoking, and real smoke coming out of his mouth. The noise alone was deafening. The traffic jams, the huge buildings, the policemen directing traffic and whistling – all this was flying by. Travel on the highway, over elevated

144

roadways, through underpasses, all this at dizzying speed! Victor tried to point out the sights, but I could not take it all in.

He then took us to the Hotel Marseille. It was a large older-style hotel: it had probably seen better days, but it looked wonderfully luxurious to me. It had an enormously large entrance hall and lounge, and our room was spacious and bright. Victor asked us to become acquainted with the place and to register with our sponsoring agency there until he would pick us up later in the day.

After a relaxing shower, which was heavenly – a shower all to ourselves with an endless supply of hot water – we joined the throngs of people on Broadway exploring our new world. We marvelled at the variety and abundance of fruit displayed in neatly stacked mountains in small delicatessen and grocery stores. The enormous variety of meat and fish and cold cuts on display. The abundance of restaurants and banks. The newspaper kiosks and the shoe-shine stands, the barber shops and laundries with their Chinese proprietors.

We had an early supper at our hotel which was supplied by our sponsor. Victor and his wife Bessie picked us up in the evening and took us to a Horn and Hardart Cafeteria for dessert and drinks. Victor gave us a lesson on how one bought food there. The variety was so plentiful we had difficult choices to make between all kinds of strange fruits like melon and grapefruit and pineapple, and the many cakes and pies and ice creams, eclairs and cream puffs. It was dizzying. Portions of these wonderful goodies were stored in small compartments with glass doors. The correct change deposited in a slot would unlock the door of one's selection. There was no end to new and novel things to amaze us.

The following day, Albert Eising paid me a visit at the hotel. He had already found a job as a delivery boy for a small grocery store. He told me that the 'Help Wanted' column in the *New York Times* was very useful for job-seekers.

I duly bought a paper and saw an advertisement in it for a nanny. There was a date and time for the interview. The address was an impressive-looking office building in Midtown Manhattan. I took my first subway ride without a hitch. I was tempted by one of the many vending machines attached to the metal columns on the platform. I think my penny bought a small piece of Hershey chocolate or a piece of Wrigley's chewing gum or chiclets. While riding the subway I became convinced that everybody was chewing gum, I was also persuaded that all American women painted their fingernails red, and I made a mental note to buy red nail polish. I was very conscious of my accent and I wanted to look and behave like an American.

The interview was held at the offices of a large concern. A secretary asked me to enter the spacious reception area where about 20 black women were waiting. I was the only white applicant. After a lengthy wait, I was the last person to be called into a private, richly furnished office, where a beautiful, elegantly dressed, dark-haired woman of about 30 greeted me. She asked me whether I had ever taken care of children before. Had I ever held a job as a nanny? I told her about my work with children in Theresienstadt and Deggendorf. She hired me on the spot – she was anxious to replace as soon as possible a nanny who had left her. We agreed that I would take a train to Hewlitt, Long Island, and then call her to be picked up at the railway station there a few days hence.

(At the time I did not question her motives for hiring me over all those black applicants. I certainly felt that I had the qualifications and experience for the job.)

Victor and Bessie Adler had owned a thriving chocolate factory in Düsseldorf. They were even more successful with their factory and store on Upper Broadway in New York City. All their candies were hand-dipped and decorated. I especially remember one large, heavy middle-aged woman in their factory. She would dip each piece of candy, which she took off a conveyor belt-like set-up, into a flowing chocolate mixture, her fingers dripping with this delicious smelling brown goo. She finished each piece beautifully, like little works of art with all kinds of designs. Her speed was amazing, and each piece of that particular batch looked perfect. The finished tray of chocolates was then refrigerated and put into boxes.

Bessie was very adept at packaging and tying exquisite bows to adorn the attractive *bonbonnières* and exhibiting them in their store window and at trade shows. They had also developed an innovative, profitable sideline of diabetic and dietetic chocolates.

The Adlers had two children, a son and a daughter. Their son Karl-Heinz, who was called Charles, was a few years older than me. He was a self-assured young man, who took me for a ride in his father's car, and showed me some of the New York sights like Macy's Department Store with its innumerable floors, escalators and elevators, eye-catching neon advertisements, and endless varieties of everything one could wish for, providing one had the money to buy it. I felt as if I was walking in a screen set.

Bessie Adler took my mother to the doctor, who confirmed the diagnosis made in Bremen, but fortunately her gall-bladder was not giving her any trouble at that time. She suffered from hot flushes and she asked the doctor to give her something to alleviate that annoying condition. She translated the term literally from German into English: 'Doctor, I am suffering terribly from the flying heat!' (*Fliegende Hitze*). She never lived that down. I understood from Bessie Adler that her doctor added that expression to his medical terminology.

We were walking in the neighbourhood of the hotel when we passed one of the many small Chinese laundry establishments. My mother pointed to the sign 'Laundry' and pronounced with conviction in her voice: 'This Mr Laundry must be very wealthy! His stores are everywhere!'

The Adlers lived above 180th Street in Upper Manhattan near Fort Tryon Park on Bennett Avenue. Shortly before I had to start my new job in Hewlitt, Long Island, they invited us to their apartment to have dinner with them. I met their daughter Ilse, who was attending high school or college at that time. She impressed me as a studious, bright young lady, and it made me a little sad that I did not have the same opportunities to go to school.

22 • Nanny, Stitcher and Waitress

The day was approaching when I had to leave for Long Island. The Adlers assured me that they would look after my mother while I was away, and they kept their promise. I followed the travel instructions carefully, and took the Long Island railway to Hewlitt. I think I arrived there on a Saturday morning.

The gentleman of the house where I was to start my job, picked me up. He was a good-looking man in his late thirties, of medium height, with an athletic build. His demeanour, his manner of speech was that of an educated, cultured man. He greeted me kindly, and drove me in his large black oldsmobile to their estate. We passed many mansions with carefully clipped hedges and park-like lawns. The wealth of the whole area through which we drove was overwhelming to my eyes; it was also incomprehensible to me that a single family could afford to live in one of those large imposing residences.

When we drove through the gate into his estate with its huge grounds, its large three-storeyed main building with a striped canvas-covered patio, sun room, auxiliary buildings, greenhouses, garages, rose garden, flower beds and magnificent trees, I wondered how I would fit into all this.

I found myself at the entrance of the main house with my one suitcase, which he had carried for me. When his wife greeted me, I thought she looked stunningly beautiful in her sporty black and white striped dress and low-heeled shoes. She immediately introduced me to Esther. Esther was a large, impressive-looking black woman, with snow-white teeth and a big smile. Esther was the cook, and as I learned later, Esther was in charge of the entire household. There were two children, Lewis, a cute, spoiled two-year-old boy and his older sister Elaine, who at the age of seven already knew how to treat people arrogantly.

I shared a large room with Lewis. My job was effectively a 24-hour shift. I had the responsibility for his food, clothing, sleeping, entertainment and general well-being. I soon found out that Lewis did not allow me uninterrupted sleep, or even ten minutes respite from my duties.

Monday morning brought the arrival of a young black woman who was Esther's helper. She was responsible for all the cleaning and washing and ironing. She dressed in colourful summer cottons, wore glossy red lipstick and her very long fingernails were covered with bright red nail-polish. She had a squeaky voice accompanied by a constant laugh. Gardeners tended the hedges, flower gardens and grounds.

The lady and gentleman of the house took their meals in the informal dining room. I ate in the large kitchen with Lewis, Elaine and Esther. I had only been there a few days when Elaine informed me that I had no right to tell her anything since I was only a servant! The only one who would not tolerate any nonsense from her was Esther. She was listened to and respected by everybody in that household.

Soon after my arrival, Esther had invited me to have a talk with her in the evening when Lewis was temporarily asleep. She asked me a lot of questions – she wanted to learn all about me. Afterwards she told me in her direct way: 'This is no place for you, you need an education! Now look at me, that's different, this lady doesn't know how to boil water, without me she would be lost! I am my own boss, I make good money, I have my room and board, and I save almost all I make. In not too many years, I'll be "the lady" in Jamaica!' Esther had an adopted daughter who was studying music at a New York City conservatory. She would play the piano on her many visits to the house.

We frequently went to the beach club, where I would play with, console and watch Lewis, while his mother would socialize and lunch with her equally wealthy friends who had also brought their maid or governess. After several hours at the club we would do the shopping in small specialized grocery and butcher's shops in Far Rockaway. The food would then be delivered to the house.

On one such shopping trip, I had developed such a craving

for some of the delicious fruits on display that I decided to buy some for myself. I had not tasted any fruit since starting my job in Hewlitt. There was always fruit in the refrigerator, as a rule it was beautifully arranged to be served in the dining room, or offered to guests at their parties. I was never offered any, and I certainly would not have helped myself. Bananas were usually ripening in the kitchen 'for Lewis'.

Esther disapproved of me spending my own money on any food, she felt strongly that it was part of my board, and she saw to it that I was told so by my employer. I still felt more comfortable filling up on all kinds of fruit on my day off which I spent in Manhattan visiting my mother.

On one of my days off while I was in the city, I opened my first bank account at the Franklin Savings Bank. I proudly showed the passbook to my mother. She had bartered some jewellery for a $100 American dollar bill while we were still in Deggendorf. We had never seen or even touched American paper money before. We treasured it – it was our most valuable possession – but soon we began to worry whether it was genuine or counterfeit. Could we get into trouble if we tried to use it or deposit it in a bank in the United States?

Exhilaration quickly turned into uneasiness. I was most apprehensive when on one of my subsequent visits into Manhattan I stopped at the Franklin Savings Bank to deposit the $100 bill. How relieved I was when the friendly teller handed my passbook back to me clearly showing a credit of $100. We almost felt rich.

The separation from my mother was troubling me and I voiced my concern about it to my employer who suggested a job for her as a housekeeper and cook in a neighbouring community where one of her acquaintances was looking for a suitable person in her household. My mother was interviewed and promptly started her new job. Her employer worked in the real-estate business. Their manners, the house, the decor were all typically *nouveau riche*. My mother was expected to cook, wash and clean the large house. She was not even given enough time to eat her meals. Her room was located on the top floor of the house. It was unbearably hot, with little ventilation and of course no air conditioning or fan. Mosquitoes were so abundant, they robbed her of her sleep. She was very unhappy there.

One morning Lewis's mother drove us (Elaine was in summer day-camp) to a place unknown to me, called Brooklyn to visit her parents' home. I don't know if Lewis's father was Jewish, but his mother came from a typically middle-class Jewish family, who lived in a nice, small urban house in a street where houses were built fairly close together. It became obvious to me that she had married into a very different world from that of her parents. I liked his grandmother, she treated me as a fellow human being, almost like a member of the family, but certainly not as a servant. It was natural for her to serve lunch for everybody in the dining room including Lewis and myself. She served Blintze (thin pancakes filled with cottage cheese and fruit) and other favourite Jewish dishes to the delight of her guests. I never met the grandfather, but Lewis's mother must have got her looks from him or some other ancestor.

One particular week started with a cupboard and storage clean-up. It began with the closets on the third floor of the house. Huge heaps of beautiful clothing and shoes were discarded. I was caught trying on a pair of brown and white loafers which fitted perfectly. She gathered everything together, I don't know if she threw it out or gave it to some charity, but when I asked her for the shoes she gave them to me reluctantly. I made some remark about the lovely dresses and blouses, skirts and sweaters and coats, but it became quite clear to me that she did not want her little boy's nanny going around in her clothes.

I wrote some poetry and some essays, and naïvely I thought that she might want to read them. I approached her one day while she was working at her desk, I showed her my writing, but it quickly became plain to me that she did not care about my past, or what had happened to my family, or my future, or my interests. I had only one friend in that house and that was Esther, who kept repeating to me: 'Child, you got to get out of here, this is no place for you. You got to get an education, you are wasting your time here, and you got to get your Mom out of that house for sure!'

I wrote to Louis Lowy, my friend from Theresienstadt who had survived the camps. He had married Ditta Jedlinsky, who had also lived at L414 in Theresienstadt before being deported to Auschwitz. They had left Deggendorf in one of the first groups allowed to enter the United States. Louis and Ditta were living in Dorchester, a suburb of Boston. He answered by return of post: 'Come to Boston, we can't help you materially or financially; however, we can give you moral support, and you'll be close to friends!'

I called my sponsors AJDC, and asked their permission to relocate to Boston. They gladly granted my request because too many new immigrants were staying in the New York area where they had arrived. In fact they were actively trying to persuade people to settle elsewhere in the country.

My leaving was not accepted graciously. The lady was quite upset and told me that I had let her down. She added: 'This is a terrible time for you to leave me. I am pregnant, I am not feeling well, I shall definitely complain to B'nai B'rith about you; they vouched for you!' She felt that when I accepted the job I entered into a commitment to work for her as long as she needed me.

Esther was happy that I was doing something 'to improve myself'. She embraced me and showered me with good wishes, and she admonished me 'to take good care of my mother'. Lewis's father took me to the railway station and wished me well.

My mother had also left her employer, and she and I took the train to Boston. A friendly woman from AJDC waited for us on the station platform. She drove us in her car to Roxbury, a part of the greater Boston area which had a large Jewish population.

AJDC had rented a room for us with a widowed lady in her mid-sixties, who owned a two-storey house. Born in Poland, she had come to the United States as a young woman. She kept a strictly kosher home. Our room came with kitchen privileges, but using her kitchen or cooking there turned into a nightmare for us. She watched every move we made, criticized any food we bought, demanded that we soak chicken for several hours in a salt water solution in her kitchen sink to make it 100 per cent kosher. She tried to force us to buy from her butcher and grocer. (These are just some examples of our everyday encounters with her!) Of course we had to keep dairy and meat products separate. She would constantly reproach us in her whiney voice, even robbing us of the little privacy the one room could have afforded us.

We got to know a neighbour who lived across the street from us, he owned a blouse factory in the Boston garment district. He knew that we were looking for jobs. (Some well-meaning person had given us hints on how to find a job in America: 'No matter what kind of job they offer you, they always want experience! If they ask you: Have you done this before?, you always answer "yes", even if you don't have the slightest idea what it is all about. That is how it's done here. That is how you get experience!') So when the friendly neighbour and owner of the Sheryl Blouse Company asked us if we had any experience working with power sewing machines, we enthusiastically replied 'yes', even though we had never seen one, never mind operated one. Two days later we found ourselves in a garment factory loft in downtown Boston, the newest employees of the Sheryl Blouse Company. I had to operate a power sewing machine stitching blouses, while my mother worked on a pinking machine (a sewing machine which sews and finishes a seam in a zigzag cut).

One operator would stitch only sleeves, another collars, while another would put the sleeves into the blouse, etc. Speed, of course, was paramount if one wanted to make any money at all. Also, since the factory worked on a piece-work basis, it was important to move the garment as quickly as possible from one operator to the other. A 'slow poke' in the chain would deprive a skilled seamstress of a constant supply of work, and therefore, of the greatest possible quantity of pieces, robbing them of earning maximum pay. The system operated on the principle of the assembly line, designed for each set of workers to put the utmost pressure on their fellow workers.

The forelady explained the machine to me, and gave me a

bundle of collars to stitch. Most of my fellow workers were young women in their twenties and early thirties. The thin olive-complexioned girl facing me, whose machine was abutting mine, had large, dark eyes, long black curly hair, and her lips and nails were painted bright red. Her name was Gerty; she was an Italian woman in her twenties. She was enormously fast and very skilled, her fingers seemed to be literally flying while her machine was racing along. She kept a careful tally of every bundle she finished.

Flanking me on one side was the daughter of the forelady, a girl in her late teens, on the other side was the sample-maker, a very able Portuguese seamstress. It took these women only a few minutes to assess my abilities. They were very decent to me, they helped me and taught me as much as their time allowed. Of course, I was holding them up, and one might argue that it was in their interest to get me going.

My mother's neighbour and co-worker, a large, mean-spirited, flabby woman in her fifties, whose bloated face and cloudy eyes gave testimony that life had probably not been kind to her, showed no inclination to help her, but instead did not miss any opportunity to keep the forelady informed of my mother's ineptness. My poor mother had a terrible time because her thread kept breaking, and not a soul came to her aid to solve her problem. I will always remember my co-workers' goodwill, especially Gerty's humanity.

The talk around the machines was mostly about money, clothes, movie stars and buying on credit, and a bit of dirt about the bosses and the forelady (when her daughter was not within earshot). Gerty had a few 'budget accounts', which allowed her to pay off her debts in small instalments over a period of time. Since that was the only way for them to afford anything, interest charges were never even mentioned. I got a lesson on how one furnishes one's apartment 'on budget'. Most of these girls were constantly in debt – as soon as one account was paid off, a new one was opened.

We started work very early in the morning, and we usually bought our lunch at the little canteen in the basement of the factory building. It was essentially a large counter with round counter stools in front of it. A middle-aged Jewish couple ran this very busy little hole in the wall. Sarah's rolls and bagels were delicious and her prices were very low. The building housed many factories. A fair number of workers bought their breakfast, lunch, coffee and cigarettes on credit. Sarah had to keep track of everybody's debts in her little book. I wonder how often she was not paid, especially since these jobs were not secure and there was always a large turnover of workers.

We very soon got used to everybody being on a first-name basis, even with the boss's son Harry who had taken over the management of the factory. Gerty and some of the other girls were sniggering when she warned me: 'Come Christmas time, Harry will probably arrange a big party here in the loft again, like last year with lots of liquor. This year I won't come, the fooling around and the goings on were terrible. He is a playboy. He is not like his father. He has a family but you would never know it. He spends most of his time travelling to Hollywood. He has big ideas!'

A few days later I was introduced to Harry – a portly, short, reddish-blond man in his mid-thirties who liked to dress in a flashy style, showing off his heavy gold watch and bracelet and rings. He mumbled some acknowledgement, but his eyes were elsewhere, and I am sure that my existence never penetrated his brain. He was excitedly discussing his idea to put the face of a popular male Hollywood film star, whom he had befriended, on some of the blouses. He believed this would be a huge success. He spent an enormous amount of money on his ideas, with dire consequences.

We found life with our landlady extremely unpleasant, so our sponsoring agency located a small apartment for us with a couple at 1 Wyoming Street in Roxbury, practically around the corner from where we had been living. Our apartment was an extended attic on the third floor of their house. Our new landlord worked as a butcher, and his wife repaired and sewed furs in her house for several of the Boston furriers.

We bought a very cheap rug and some dishes and other necessities. We tried to spend as little money as possible, looking for sales. The meaning of that magic word was one of the first things my mother fully comprehended, and her delight when she found a bargain never diminished.

We had no telephone and so we could only be reached by calling our landlord. The agency paid our rent for a number of months. Our landlord, however, claimed that he had not been paid, and one day he came up to our apartment ranting and raving, threatening to throw us out. It turned out that indeed, he had been paid; he tried to justify his behaviour, but the whole episode soured the good feelings between us.

Mrs Goldschmidt, her son Jochem and her daughter Eva, who had been in the DP camp in Deggendorf with us, had also relocated to the Boston area. They came to visit us at 1 Wyoming Street. My mother and I were overwhelmed by their gift of a most beautiful bouquet of gladioli. Such luxury! The Goldschmidts enventually returned to New York City.*

About this time my mother suffered a bad gall-bladder attack and was admitted on an emergency basis to Beth Israel hospital. Since the doctors could not determine with certainty whether she had an acute appendix or a gall-bladder which was ready to rupture, they decided to remove both organs. She had a fairly lengthy hospital stay but she recovered fully. Her gall-bladder attack also finished her stitching career at Sheryl Blouse Company. After her recuperation she found the ideal job as hostess and organizer of board-member luncheons and parties at a branch of a national Jewish philanthropic organization in Boston.

Louis Lowy had a friend whose brother had just returned from duty as a paratrooper in the Pacific. At his friend's urging he arranged a blind date for me with this young man. So one evening Mr Stieglitz picked me up in his gleaming black oldsmobile. I was impressed. I thought his conversation a bit strange during our drive which took us to the Boston Harbor area, where he took me into a crowded, smoky night club, alive with rowdy, drunken sailors and garishly dressed girls. I didn't quite know how to extricate myself from this very uncomfortable situation. I had that helpless feeling of being trapped slowly rising in me while he was ordering Manhattan cocktails for us.

Suddenly police whistles were blowing from everywhere

---

*The world is a small place: as we learned later, the Goldschmidts are actually cousins of my husband.

like fire crackers. The place was being raided and with the help of my escort I found myself escaping through a window. He apologized for getting me into such a predicament; I kept my composure, but asked him firmly to take me home, which he did. I called Louis and Ditta and impressed on them never to pair me up with anybody on a blind date again!

The Sheryl Blouse Company filed for bankruptcy in late 1947. All the employees including myself went to the court house to file our grievances since the company still owed us wages. I filled out forms as instructed, but never received a penny of the money they owed me. My status was referred to as being laid off. I scanned all the 'Help Wanted' ads in the newspaper and I was interviewed by several other manufacturers in the garment district, without success.

My mother and I attended a gathering of the IMAS (Immigrant Mutual Aid Society), a Jewish-German refugee club founded in Boston in the 1930s. The original members were of my mother's age, but their children had formed their own groups within this organization. That made it an important social outlet for people of my age as well. We met people there and we made friends. My mother had a new social base and people her age were reaching out to her. I think that this contributed greatly to her enthusiasm and love of life in her new surroundings. She adjusted quickly and she wanted to learn English, and become an active participant in her newly adopted country.

Since I had lost my job at the Sheryl Blouse Company I was desperately looking for new employment. We became good friends with a couple we had met at the IMAS: the husband had a managerial position at the headquarters of a restaurant chain in Boston. He arranged an interview for me with the manager of one of their restaurants in the city and I was offered a job to wait at table, or work behind the counter, or wherever I was needed.

These eateries were cheap breakfast, lunch and dinner places – the forerunners of the fast-food culture. This restaurant had a long counter and small tables as well. It was a busy place, and most of the customers worked nearby in the downtown business area of the city. Speed was all-important in this job.

The waiters and short-order cooks were a coarse lot: they had their own lingo, 95 per cent of which I did not comprehend. I had never heard of abbreviations like 'BLT' for bacon, lettuce and tomato sandwich, 'no mayo', 'pie *à la mode*', 'eggs over light', to name just a few of the expressions which had not been covered in my English lessons. I had never worked in a restaurant before, and I felt totally lost. I did not find another 'Gerty' there; nobody was helpful, nobody guided me. There was a cut-throat atmosphere among the employees. I cannot recall how long I lasted there, but I do remember that my tenure was very brief.

At that time I often wondered whether I would ever find a good satisfying job. Because my education had been severely disrupted I could not produce impressive certificates of learned accomplishments, or even the basic requirements for most jobs. I was still dreaming of somehow becoming a doctor. As I have mentioned earlier, it had been my wish ever since I met those two women on the way from Düsseldorf to Theresienstadt: one a radiologist and the other a nurse. I don't know what happened to those two women who touched my life for such a brief period of time but who made a lasting impression on me.

23 · Siegmund

A social worker of our sponsoring agency told us that English language classes were available at a Jewish synagogue in Brookline. She made it clear to my mother that they were specifically structured for new immigrants.

I enrolled my mother in the beginners' class and I took an advanced course in their evening school. After classes, some of the ladies of the synagogue arranged a social get-together, where they served coffee and cake, and encouraged the students to get to know each other. They would respond to our questions and they would try to be helpful in any way they could to ease our adjustment to a new life and a new language.

At one of these events I was sure that I recognized a tall gentleman as the father of one of my former schoolmates in Düsseldorf. He and his son shared an uncanny likeness, I thought. I introduced myself and asked him: 'Are you by any chance the father of Hannelore and Herbert Bruenell?' (His daughter Hannelore had been in my brother's class and his son Herbert was a year ahead of me.)

Siegmund Bruenell was so very happy to meet me and my mother. He cried like a child. All his pent-up grief flowed from him. He had just arrived in the United States from Shanghai. After Kristallnacht in 1938 the Nazis gave him an ultimatum: to leave Germany immediately or be imprisoned! He escaped via the trans-Siberian railway and ended up in China. His wife Hertha, his son Herbert and his daughter Hannelore had all been killed by the Nazis. Siegmund Bruenell was temporarily living with his brother and sister-in-law in Brookline. This was indeed the beginning of a 'beautiful friendship'. I think Siegmund fell in love with my mother that very evening in the adult school.

Siegmund was selling Fuller Brushes and household articles door-to-door. He carried a sample case and catalogues. Armed with a ready smile and a good personality, he often found an open door. He was a natural salesman, and his strong accent only seemed to enhance his appeal. Unintentionally using the wrong phrases or vocabulary with often hilarious results was his most successful sales-pitch. His customers would give him an order for items they picked out of the catalogue; they would make a downpayment, and a delivery date with the payment of the balance was arranged.

Siegmund had no inventory. He would fill his orders at the nearest Fuller Brush outlet. Many newly arrived immigrants started out as door-to-door salesmen as he did. To help deliver his orders, he bought a used 1937 Ford. It had a rumble seat with a spare tyre fastened to it and running boards under the doors. My mother and I were the beneficiaries of his new acquisition.

Siegmund was a constant visitor to our apartment at 1 Wyoming Street in Roxbury. His newly acquired car made these visits a lot easier. He went out of his way to chauffeur my mother around, and could not do enough for her. He was obviously courting her. She liked him and she liked the attention, but her heart was still with my father.

24 · X-ray

I think it was in late December 1947 when we were called to the phone by our landlord. The caller identified herself as Gustel Morton. She told me that her mother's maiden name was Lenneberg and that all Lennebergs are related. She went on to explain that one or several New York newspapers regularly published names of survivors and new immigrants who had arrived in New York, and that her mother Pauline Schreiber, *née* Lenneberg, had seen our name on one of those lists. Her mother was living in New York City at that time, and she had called her because she had tried to contact us herself but was informed that we had relocated to Boston. Gustel Morton arranged for us to meet her and her husband Martin a few days later.

The Mortons picked us up in their elegant black Oldsmobile and drove us to their luxurious apartment in Cambridge. (Gustel and Martin Morton had emigrated to America in 1932 or 1933.) Martin had an import–export business dealing mostly with India. Gustel had been an artist for the better part of her life. She worked in ceramics, wood and metal, and she painted mostly in oils. Gustel's brother, George Schreiber, was a well-known artist. (I think it was Gustel's life-long ambition to match her brother's success, which unfortunately eluded her.)

The Mortons' apartment was filled with paintings and other works of art, exotic plants and flowers and cacti in all shapes and forms. The walls were lined with bookcases and the floors were covered with oriental rugs. Most of their furniture was of Scandinavian design in blond or light-brown fruit wood. This was a very different world from our attic apartment at 1 Wyoming Street in Roxbury or the Sheryl Blouse Company.

Martin was tall and well-built, with dark curly hair greying at the temples. He was socially adept, assertive and skilful in handling people. Both Gustel and Martin were about forty. Gustel dressed and acted like the artist she was and aspired to be recognized as. She mostly wore trousers when few women dared to do so. She even wore them to formal parties, and loved to show off her slender figure in them. Her straight blonde hair fell loosely not quite touching her shoulders. She was seldom seen without a cigarette in a long holder. (She was a chain-smoker all her life.) She loved all things exotic.

Gustel and Martin led an active social life. Their guests and friends were intellectuals and professionals, mostly physicians and professors – a good number of them German-born Jewish immigrants. The Mortons owned a summer home on a lake in North Conway, New Hampshire, to which they invited many of their friends. The parties at their retreat were a favourite topic of conversation amongst their guests.

Gustel and Martin invited us to a social get-together, where we met many of their friends. (In retrospect I am sure that it was solely arranged for my benefit.) Among the people present were Dr Alice Ettinger, Chief Radiologist at Pratt Diagnostic Hospital (better known as New England Medical Center); Dr Anna Reinauer, of the same hospital, and her sister Eva, the chief radiologist at the Boston Dispensary (also part of the same medical complex); a professor of languages from Wheaton College; a urologist from Beth Israel Hospital; Philip and Gertrude Mendel (very close friends of the Mortons, in their sixties at that time); and most importantly we met the lady responsible for our good fortune, Gustel Morton's mother Pauline who had come to visit from New York City. She and my mother took an immediate liking to each other and their friendship lasted for a long time, indeed until Pauline's death.

For me the social evening turned into a series of interviews with different people. They all took a low-key approach to their questioning of me. They were considerate and they made me feel completely at ease. They wanted to know what I wanted to do with my life and what I wanted to learn? When I told Dr Ettinger that I had always wanted to become a doctor, and particularly a radiologist, she was sympathetic but assured me with Gustel that that was not feasible at that time considering my background. Dr Ettinger must have been amused by my naïvety but she did not show it; on the contrary, she took my hopes and dreams very seriously and skilfully guided me into thinking about related options in the medical field that would be realistically attainable for me.

I had mentioned to Gustel in previous conversations that I especially liked the study of languages and, of course, medicine. She had obviously chosen her guest list accordingly. The professor of languages from Wheaton College also felt that I was lacking too much basic education for a college education in languages.

Dr Ettinger invited me to come and see her the following Saturday at Pratt Diagnostic Hospital in Boston. As she put it: 'We'll have another chat!' Even though I was eagerly looking forward to seeing her the following Saturday, I was nervous and worried whether I would impress her favourably and find the right answers to her questions.

Gertrude and Philip Mendel became our best friends. Philip gave English lessons to my mother. He was a great teacher and my mother was an eager student whose language skills improved like magic. This helped her enormously to become attuned to a new country with an unfamiliar language and different customs.

Gertrude was a music teacher and a pianist. I enjoyed our visits to their house. Gertrude taught me Stephen Foster songs and I loved to sing with her when she accompanied us on the piano. Philip and Gertrude had an only son, who was a professor of music at Princeton University. They were very proud of his appointment, but back then the name Princeton did not mean anything to me. The Mendels often asked us to have dinner with them and we became part of their family. We were still living in Roxbury at 1 Wyoming Street, but somehow we felt optimistic. Doors were starting to open to us, and we were sure that we would make a better life for ourselves.

It was about this time that I started to go to concerts. For many years after the war Beethoven's music stirred me so very deeply. I cannot explain why it overwhelmed and upset me, but it caused so many repressed feelings to well up in me that I would cry uncontrollably. I was drawn to it but it devastated me. I vividly remember this happening at a concert in Boston. I, and another young woman, attended a concert of Beethoven's Ninth Symphony (we were the guests of some university students who were in Boston from leave on a kibbutz). I felt embarrassed, but I was unable to control my feelings. I did not listen to Beethoven's music for a very long time after that incident. (I overcame this difficulty only much later.)

Pratt Diagnostic Hospital was part of an impressive medical complex. The major teaching hospital of Tufts Medical School, this centre included the Floating Hospital for Children and the Boston Dispensary for outpatients and indigents.

When I entered the front lobby of this modern, bright, impressive building, I was not aware that I was going to see one of the most famous radiologists in the country. I took the elevator to the X-ray Department which was practically deserted this Saturday afternoon, except for one technician on call at the front desk. It was a huge department which occupied an entire floor of this enormous complex. I found the door to which I had been directed by the technician: the name plate on it said: Alice Ettinger, MD. Dr Ettinger greeted me warmly. She immediately made me feel at ease. She was an impressive woman of above average height, with very intelligent, kind eyes. Her posture gave evidence of a marked kypholordosis (backward curvature) of the spine. She wore a long white coat and her eyeglasses were dangling from a black cord around her neck.

She did not quiz me, but she immediately took charge of the conversation. 'Ursula, I think I got a pretty good idea about your preferences when we talked at Gustel and Martin's. I think you have the potential to become a capable X-ray technician. You are lacking many prerequisites, so please don't discuss your lack of schooling with anybody. Students are not paid for their work while in training, but I shall arrange some compensation for you. In return you would be expected to work at the Boston Dispensary X-ray Department under the supervision of Eva Reinauer, the head technician there. The hours will be determined by her after your daily training and class schedule here at Pratt

Diagnostic, under the head technologist Mr Ralph Bannister. In addition to a salary for your work you will also get free meal tickets and free laundry service for your uniforms. Please don't discuss this either. You might want to think my offer over; however, if you agree to my conditions and offer, you can report to Mr Bannister at 7 a.m. on Monday morning. He will instruct you on what you have to wear: uniforms, white stockings and shoes, etc.'

I could hardly believe my ears and I wanted to pinch myself to make sure that I was not dreaming! I had expected to leave with some good advice, but not with an offer to start my training a few days hence. I thanked Dr Ettinger and assured her that I did not need to think it over, and I accepted her offer directly and gratefully.

She immediately treated me like a member of her staff, and spent the rest of the afternoon showing me each room of her department and explaining its function. I saw the impressive, large X-ray machines with their many controls and 'gadgets', and cones of various sizes; the automatic, moving X-ray tables. She put one into a vertical position by just stepping on a foot switch! She explained the necessity of protecting oneself from any radiation with lead-lined aprons and gloves. She showed me a film badge which everybody in the department had to wear at all times making sure that nobody received any X-ray exposure. She also wanted me to understand that any members of her staff who exposed themselves carelessly would face immediate dismissal. She added: 'You see the badge tells me the story; please keep that in mind and follow all the safety rules which Mr Bannister will outline to you on Monday!'

She showed me the units for special procedures, the mobile units which are used at bedside and in the operating room, the darkroom complex, the film drying area, the staff radiologists' reading room, the gastro-intestinal and barium enema suites, and so on. I tried to absorb as much as I could of her descriptions and explanations, but everything soon became a blur.

This was a medical science world I did not even know existed when I had entered the lobby of this centre only a few hours before, and now I was going to be part of it! Doubts of my ability to tackle the tasks ahead of me never entered my mind. I was determined and I was not afraid to work very hard. Dr Ettinger concluded the tour by personally showing me some other parts of the centre touching on its history and mission.

I left the hospital lobby in a daze. I walked along Bennet Street, around the many buildings of the hospitals and Tufts Medical School and I was still wondering whether this was really happening to me. I finally made it back to Roxbury. My mother, Siegmund and I celebrated with a bottle of wine in our attic apartment.

Mr Bannister, the head technologist and chief of the training programme, was a good teacher. He was a capable and fair man and well-disposed toward me. He taught me everything about X-ray technique that I needed to learn. He was always accessible and ready to explain and demonstrate, no matter how much time it took or at what time of day the questions were presented to him. I was so fortunate to be working under excellent technicians: some of them like Pat Whitehurst became my very good friends.

I started work at 7 a.m. at Pratt Diagnostic and after I finished there at 3 p.m., I would cross the street to the Boston Dispensary or the Floating Children's Hospital and work with Eva Reinauer and her staff in the X-ray Department there as long as I was needed, which was usually until 6 p.m. I would then return to Roxbury and often use my poor mother as a guinea pig: practising positioning techniques on her hands, arms, feet, legs, spine and head. My double shifts and insatiable appetite to learn did not escape Dr Ettinger's notice, and she told me years later that I was the best student she had ever had.

Pratt Diagnostic was a prestigious institution, we had many famous patients such as Raoul Dufy, the painter, Serge Koussevitsky the conductor, politicians and wealthy industrialists. Dufy was suffering from severe crippling rheumatoid arthritis. He was treated with cortisone in the drug's early miracle stage, and his recovery was so dramatic that the doodles on his paper placemats depicted him coming into the hospital in a wheelchair with crutches by his bedside and leaving the hospital, walking out of the lobby unattended. (I wish I had understood who Dufy was at that time, as I could easily have got hold of one of those placemats!)

Howard Johnson was also a patient at our hospital while I was there. He showed his gratitude to the interns and residents by presenting them with green ties with the logo of Simon the pieman embroidered on them. Most of the doctors did not appreciate his generosity.

Shortly after I started my training, Siegmund surprised me with the thoughtful gift of Saunders 1947 edition of the *American Medical Dictionary*. I am sure he had to sell a lot of Fuller Brushes to pay for it.

25 · Married

In early August of 1948, Louis* telephoned me and invited me to his house, he added: 'There will also be somebody here who is interested in X-rays.' I reminded him that I myself was only a student and that I had no influence to get anybody accepted into the programme at Pratt Diagnostic. He assured me that he was aware of that.

I was left with the impression that Louis and Ditta were giving a party and that one of their guests would be interested in becoming an X-ray technician.

The only guest at their house on that evening was a handsome young man. Hans Pawel was of medium height, slim, with black wavy hair and intelligent, lively brown eyes. He came across as a cultured and educated person. His conversation was interesting, I shared many of his views. I felt comfortable with him and liked him a lot.

He explained to me that a distant relative of his was the famous Dr Bucky, who invented a diaphragm which was named after him and a collaborator, a Dr Potter, and which still to this day is an essential part of every X-ray table used in the world; it is referred to by X-ray staff as the 'Bucky'.

Hans was working in a machine shop. His education at the Technische Hochschule in Prague had been interrupted, but he had been fortunate enough to spend the war years in England.

When we left Louis and Ditta's house it was so late that we caught our separate last subway trains home but not before arranging a date to see each other again a few days hence.

Siegmund was delighted when Hans came into our family. He would frequently pick Hans up at his furnished room in Brookline. Now we had two regular visitors. On Saturday

*Louis and Ditta Lowy have remained our good friends. Louis was a professor of sociology at Boston University. He died in 1991.

mornings Hans would sometimes help Siegmund deliver his Fuller Brush orders to customers and boarding houses so that they could spend more time with us. He would then treat us to some deliciously funny encounters with Siegmund's customers. During one such delivery to a boarding house he overheard Siegmund offering his customer boxes of 'second-hand' toilet paper at a reduced price. What he meant to offer was second-rate paper which was sometimes slightly flawed. Hans carefully explained the difference to Siegmund, and he was surprised and puzzled when on the following Saturday he again heard him offering his second-hand toilet paper to a customer. When Hans reminded him: 'But Siegmund, I explained the difference between seconds and second-hand to you last week!' Siegmund assured him: 'I know but it helps me to sell!'

Hans and I had been dating for six weeks when we decided to get married. My mother was shocked and Siegmund was delighted. I am sure that he felt that his chance of marrying my mother had improved considerably. Dr Ettinger was not too thrilled either. She told me that getting married and having children was against her rules since these were the main reasons for losing her best technicians. Of course, she was only half-serious: in fact, she hired me as a fully fledged technician one month before I was eligible to graduate. It was a great honour for me to be hired by Dr Ettinger, but to be put on the payroll before graduation was the ultimate reward.

I worked for Dr Ettinger for three and a half years. I kept in touch with her until two or three years before her death in 1993. In 1982 she received the highest honour a radiologist can aspire to: the Gold Medal from the Radiological Society of North America. I have been told that only one other woman, namely Marie Curie, was honoured with such distinction. I will always remember this great lady, and I think of her with gratitude and admiration.

Hans and I got married on 24 September 1948. The Brookline JP, Mr Shinners, conducted the ceremony and Philip Mendel and Erwin Dallman (Hans's cousin Erna's husband) were witnesses. My mother and Siegmund married one week later.

I may at some time continue my story, but for now I end this sketch of my early days in Europe, and my new life in the New World. This great country is one of only a few which admit immigrants, and it stands alone in the full participation in society that a foreign-born citizen can enjoy. I, the newcomer, could dream and struggle and build a future like millions of others have done before, on an equal footing with those whose ancestors had long been here. I am grateful for the opportunities for a full life America has afforded me, my husband and our children. But I will always feel saddened when I reflect on what could have been if we had been allowed to come here in 1938.

As I look back on what went before – the memory of my father, and my brother, my many friends and relatives, the memory of murder and horror, the sense of lost roots and home and country – I feel that perhaps I, much more so than others, can truly realize what it means to be free, to be able to voice one's opinion, to choose to worship or not to worship. I think that those of us who were deprived of freedom truly treasure it and will never take it for granted.

Postscript

Buschi and Hannah and Zdenka were important friends in my life, so I want to give a brief account of what happened to them.

Hannah was very ill when we left her at the hospital in Trutnov (Trautenau), but fortunately she eventually recovered. Her husband did not survive the camps. She came to the United States in 1946 and married Imre Messinger in Chicago in 1947. They have a son and a daughter. Hannah is an artist. She and I remain very close friends.

Zdenka returned to Prague after liberation. Her husband also did not survive. She married Ruda Luhan, with whom she had two sons. Her family endured the Russian occupation of Czechoslovakia, and saw their country turn into a totalitarian, communist satellite. Thus she lost her freedom of expression and movement for the second time in her life.

Buschi came to the United States probably in 1948. She worked for a short time in New York City as a nanny. She bought an old car with the money she had earned, and drove by herself cross-country to Los Angeles where she eventually obtained work in the medical field. She married Ernst Freudenberg in 1952. He died of heart disease several years later.

Hannah repeatedly tried to get permission from the Czech communist authorities to enable Zdenka to visit us in America. She finally succeeded against all odds, making it possible for a reunion of Zdenka, Hannah, Buschi and me to take place at Buschi's home in Los Angeles in 1977. Buschi died one year later of cancer of the pancreas. Zdenka Luhanova was about 80 when she died in Prague.

My husband Hans Pawel retired in 1990 as a professor of mechanical engineering at a technical university. Earlier he had worked for many years in industry. He died of cancer on 3 November 1999. Both our sons and their wives have had successful professional careers. Our only grandchild Laura was born in 1993.

Siegmund was a wonderful grandfather – the only grandfather our sons have known, for both my father and my husband's parents were killed by the Nazis. Siegmund died of heart disease in 1966.

My mother Caroline (Lina) died in 1985.